THE DEATH OF CALIGULA

The Death of Caligula

Josephus *Ant. Iud.* XIX 1–273,
translation and commentary

T. P. Wiseman

LIVERPOOL UNIVERSITY PRESS

First published in 2013 by
Liverpool University Press
4 Cambridge Street
Liverpool
L69 7ZU

British Library Cataloguing-in-Publication data
A British Library CIP record is available

ISBN 978 1 84631 964 8 cased
ISBN 978 1 84631 963 1 paperback

Typeset by Carnegie Book Production, Lancaster.
Printed and bound by Bell & Bain Ltd, Glasgow

Contents

Illustrations

Acknowledgements

For helpful criticism and suggestions, I am very grateful to Tony Barrett (who greatly improved the first draft of the translation), to Tony Woodman, and to my colleagues in the Exeter Classics research seminar. They are not responsible for whatever errors and infelicities remain.

For this second edition, 22 years after the first, I have updated the bibliography, made some adjustments and additions to the introduction, translation and commentary, and completely revised Appendix 1 in the light of recent archaeological information. A new figure 2 was kindly drawn for me by András Bereznay; figures 1 and 3 were drawn for the original edition by the late Rodney Fry and by Seán Goddard respectively; figure 4 is reproduced by permission of the Ministero per i Beni e le Attività Culturali—Soprintendenza Speciale per i Beni Archeologici di Roma.

Exeter, May 2013

Dis Manibus
Cornelii Sabini
sacrum

Introduction

The Roman Republic may be said to have ended when Caesar crossed the Rubicon with his army and invaded Italy in 49 BC. He was made dictator, and after his assassination in 44 BC there was a succession of civil wars until his adopted son defeated Antony and Cleopatra and emerged in 30 BC as the sole ruler of the Roman empire. In 27 BC the young Caesar made a great show of handing power back to the Senate and People of Rome, in return for which he was given the new and honorific name of Caesar Augustus. So began the Roman principate, in theory a restored republic, in practice a disguised autocracy.

It soon became clear that Augustus intended an heir of his own blood to inherit his position. He had no son, but his daughter Julia gave him five grandchildren, three boys and two girls. Augustus adopted the boys as his own sons; but two of them died young and the other was temperamentally unsuitable to be his heir. In AD 4 (he was 65), Augustus reluctantly adopted his stepson Tiberius, the elder son of his wife Livia by her previous marriage, as his son and heir, his deputy and his designated successor.

However, one of Augustus' granddaughters was married to Tiberius' nephew Germanicus. Tiberius, no doubt at Augustus' insistence, adopted Germanicus; and so, through Germanicus' children, the succession would eventually revert to the blood descendants of Augustus himself. The essentials of the family tree are shown overleaf.

Augustus died in AD 14. Tiberius, now 55, succeeded to a position he didn't want and inherited an autocracy of which he disapproved. He would have liked to retire and leave the government of Rome to the Senate and magistrates. But he couldn't do it; as he said, he was holding a wolf by the ears and couldn't let go.[1] Germanicus, meanwhile, was in command of Rome's armies on the Rhine. His wife, Augustus' granddaughter Agrippina,

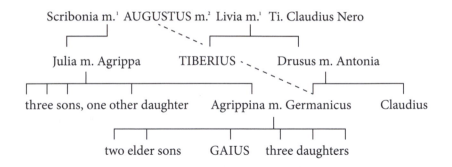

was with him, and so was their third son, Gaius Caesar, a two-year-old whose miniature army boots earned him the nickname 'Caligula'.

The tragic principate of Tiberius saw the death of Germanicus at 33 (poisoned, some said), followed by more than a decade of murderous dynastic struggle in which Agrippina and her two eldest sons were arrested for treason, exiled or imprisoned, and eventually killed. Little Gaius survived; but he spent his formative years with the embittered old Tiberius in the imperial villa on Capri. He got no training in the responsibilities of government, no experience of holding senatorial office or military command. Tiberius had no illusions about his heir: 'I am bringing up,' he said, 'a viper for the Roman People and a Phaethon for the world.'[2] It was what Augustus had planned (Gaius was his great-grandson); but for the constitutional facade of the Augustan principate it was a total disaster.

Gaius was 24 years old when Tiberius died in March 37. Not for him the devious diplomacy of Augustus or the anguished reluctance of Tiberius. He had the power and was going to use it, despotically. 'Remember,' he told his grandmother Antonia, 'I can do anything to anybody.'[3] After less than four years, the way he used his power—and the things he did to people—brought about his assassination.

Most of what we know about the appalling history of the Caesars' dynasty we know from the *Annals* of Cornelius Tacitus, which covered the period from the accession of Tiberius to the fall of Nero in 68. But the *Annals* do not survive complete; books VII and VIII, which dealt with Gaius, are missing (as are IX and X on the first six years of Claudius). Suetonius and Cassius Dio are not enough to fill the gap. The former gives fascinating personal details but no chronologically coherent narrative; the latter, writing a century later, cannot match the political grasp and insight of Tacitus. Besides, for Gaius' final year and the events that brought Claudius to power, even Dio's text is lost, and we have to rely on excerpts and summaries.

However, the loss is not irreparable. For the text of another author survives which tells us in authentic detail of the death of the emperor Gaius and its dramatic aftermath.

When the events described in this book were taking place, its author was a four-year-old boy in Jerusalem, named Joseph ben Mattathias. Over fifty years later, probably in AD 94, he wrote an autobiographical justification of his career, which began with this account of his background:[4]

> My family is not undistinguished. From a long way back it traces its descent from priests; and just as different peoples define nobility in different ways, so among us the proof of aristocratic birth is participation in the priesthood ... Moreover, I am of royal blood on my mother's side, for she was descended from the Hasmoneans, who for a long period were not only high priests of our nation, but also kings.

As a boy, according to his own account, Joseph ben Mattathias was a prodigy of learning, already at the age of fourteen being consulted by the high priests on the finer points of Jewish tradition. At sixteen he undertook a thorough course of training in all the three main sects—the Pharisees, the Sadducees and the Essenes—and followed that up with three years' discipleship to an ascetic teacher in the wilderness. 'Returning to the city in my nineteenth year, I began to conduct my life according to the rules of the Pharisees, a sect closely resembling what the Greeks call the Stoic school' (*Life* 12).

Joseph was no doubt unaware of that Greek parallel at the time. But Greek was throughout the eastern half of the Roman empire the medium of culture, government and diplomacy, and not even Jerusalem was immune to it.[5] Certainly Joseph could speak Greek fluently by the time he was 26, for in AD 64 he went on an embassy to Rome to negotiate the release of some priests who had been arrested by the procurator of Judaea. His contacts were good enough to get him introduced to Nero's empress, Poppaea Sabina, who arranged for the priests to be freed and sent Joseph home laden with goodwill gifts.[6]

Not surprisingly, when the Jewish revolt against Rome broke out two years later, Joseph argued strongly against it. But in vain—and soon he found himself in charge of the defence of Galilee against the Romans. His motives and his loyalties were bitterly disputed at the time, and have remained controversial ever since. For our purposes it is enough to report that in the spring of 67 Joseph's forces were concentrated at Jotapata; Nero's general Vespasian besieged the town and then captured it in a surprise attack; the hard core of the resistance, hiding in a cave, refused to surrender and preferred to die by their own hands; Joseph was one of the last two left alive. Unwilling, he tells us, to stain his hands with the blood of a compatriot, he talked his fellow-survivor out of the suicide pact and surrendered to the Romans.[7]

Joseph always insisted that his actions were guided from on high, by

> dreams in the night by which God had forewarned him both of the calamities coming to the Jews and of the fortunes of the Roman emperors. Moreover in the matter of interpreting dreams he was capable of divining the meaning of equivocal utterances of the Deity: he was familiar with the prophecies of holy scripture, being a priest himself and a descendant of priests.[8]

When brought before Vespasian, he prophesied that the general would soon be emperor. Vespasian kept him in chains, but decided not to send him to Nero.

Two years later, Nero was dead, his successor Galba had been assassinated, and there was civil war between the pretenders Otho and Vitellius. The eastern armies hailed Vespasian as emperor in the summer of 69. Joseph, his prophecy now on the point of coming true, was released from custody. He spent the next eighteen months with the Roman army under Vespasian's son Titus, who brought the Jewish revolt to an end with the siege and destruction of Jerusalem.

Like the Babylonians 656 years before, the Romans destroyed the Temple as agents of the wrath of God, punishing the sins of the Jews. That was how Joseph saw it, with himself in the role of Jeremiah, prophesying in vain.[9] He had not been able to prevent the catastrophe, but at least he could bear witness to what had happened. He wrote an account of the war (probably quite short) in Aramaic, for the Jews of the eastern diaspora in Parthia, Babylonia and Mesopotamia.[10]

By then he was in Rome. Titus' victorious army returned in 71, bringing with it the Jewish priest who had prophesied Vespasian's rise to power. The new emperor showed his gratitude with three valuable gifts: free lodging in one of the imperial mansions; a regular income from the imperial treasury; and the Roman citizenship.[11] Joseph ben Mattathias now becomes Flavius Josephus. (His full name was probably T. Flavius Josephus, but the *praenomen* happens not to be attested.)

He was 34, safe, subsidised, and in the enviable position of an imperial favourite. For the next twenty-five years—through the reigns of Vespasian (70–9) and his sons Titus (79–81) and Domitian (81–96)—Josephus devoted himself to writing history, and defending himself from the attacks of his many enemies.

His first major work was a history of the Jewish war, expanded from his Aramaic narrative and elaborated with all the features proper to Greek historiography. For Josephus was now writing in Greek, the international language of literary culture. The history is in seven books, the first two of which give an introductory account of the historical background from 167 BC to AD 66, including (at II 184–214) a brief narrative of the emperor Gaius' dealings with the Jews, followed by his assassination and the succession of Claudius in AD 41.

The *Jewish War* was completed about 81, and published at imperial expense with a personal endorsement from Titus ('so anxious was he that men should learn of the events from my volumes alone').[12] Josephus now turned to a more ambitious project—nothing less than the complete history of the Jews, from Adam to his own time. The *Antiquities of the Jews* are in twenty books: the first ten (essentially biblical narrative) down to the destruction of the first Temple by the Babylonians in 587 BC, books XI–XX (largely from Hellenistic sources) down to the outbreak of the revolt in 66 which led to the destruction of the third Temple by the Romans. When Josephus finished this huge work, Vespasian and Titus were both dead. He signs off at *Ant.* XX 267 'in the thirteenth year of Domitian Caesar and the fifty-sixth year of my life'—i.e. in AD 93/94.

Living in Rome in close contact with the imperial court, writing in Greek in a literary tradition that went back to Herodotus and Thucydides, Josephus was clearly well integrated into Greco-Roman culture.[13] As a historian of dramatic recent events, he will have read with particular avidity the historical works that appeared in the 70s dealing with the later Julio-Claudians and the civil wars of 68–9.

Tacitus later commented on the understandable partiality of these historians towards the new regime;[14] Josephus, who no doubt did not object to that, nevertheless criticizes their excessive hostility to Nero (*Ant.* xx 154–6). At any rate, when he decided to devote most of the nineteenth book of the *Antiquities* to the assassination of Gaius 'Caligula', as an exemplary story of divine providence, he was not short of good Roman authorities to provide him with a detailed narrative.

Who were the Flavian historians? We know of three who were conspicuous enough to be mentioned in contemporary literary works, and authoritative enough to be cited as sources by Tacitus. They are: Cluvius Rufus, a senior senator (ex-consul) who had been prominent at Nero's court but not corrupted by it;[15] Fabius Rusticus, a friend and compatriot of Seneca, probably of equestrian rank;[16] and the elder Pliny, a learned equestrian officer whose history was published after the author's death in the Vesuvius eruption of 79.[17] We can, I think, be certain that Josephus was familiar with the works of all three of them.

It has often been taken for granted, even by the best scholars, that Josephus' Gaius narrative in *Antiquities* xix is based on a single Roman source. I confess I cannot understand how that opinion could survive a close reading of the text. There are numerous doublets and inconsistencies which it seems to me can only be explained by the assumption that Josephus was working from at least two sources, and did not always succeed in combining them into a single coherent account.

Source-analysis is always an uncertain business, and I make no extravagant claims for my own version;[18] readers must judge for themselves whether or not the arguments presented in the commentary are valid. If they are, then what emerges may be tentatively summarised as shown on the opposite page.[19]

The asterisked passage (237–45) is a special case—an inserted digression from a source particularly concerned with the deeds of the Jewish King Agrippa. Leave that to one side, along with Josephus' own contributions, and the most economical hypothesis is that Josephus was using two Roman authors, one of whom (the 'main source') accounts for 179 out of the 273 sections, the other for 71. There are a few hints—an interest in Cordoba and Stoicism—which suggest that the latter may be Seneca's friend Fabius Rusticus.[20] If so, then we can attribute to him a particular hatred of Claudius' over-powerful freedmen, and a disenchanted view of the rapacity, arrogance and incompetence of senators which contrasts conspicuously with the attitude of the main source.[21]

Josephus himself	Main source	Other source(s)
1		
		2–14
15–16		
		17–23
	24–61	
61		
	62–67	
68–69		
	70–93	
		94–95
	96–105	
106–108		
	109–157	
		158–160
	161–196	
196–198		
	198–211	
		212–236
		237–245*
		246–268
	269–273	

The main source himself (wrongly, I think, supposed to be the *only* source) was identified by Theodor Mommsen in 1870 as Cluvius Rufus, whose comment is quoted in the scene in the theatre (92). Sir Ronald Syme was more cautious, and suggested the possibility of Servilius Nonianus.[22] But that is very unlikely: Servilius died in 59, and if there is one thing we can be sure of about Josephus' main source, it is that he was looking back at the events of 41 with the hindsight of one who had lived through the last years of Nero and the civil wars that followed.[23] The detectable allusions to the events of 68–9,[24] and the roles assigned to persons (or the forebears of persons) who were significant in the Flavian period,[25] make it as certain as can be that the date of composition was some time in the 70s. I believe Mommsen was right; but since the evidence for Cluvius Rufus involves a somewhat intricate argument, I have dealt with it separately in Appendix 2.

Fortunately for us, Josephus stuck pretty closely to his Roman sources (even traces of their Latin may sometimes be detected in his Greek).[26] But he did not simply transcribe them. He added explanatory notes for his non-Roman audience,[27] and he went out of his way to remind his Greek readers that he was a historian in the tradition of Thucydides.[28] In the preface (15) he claims the Thucydidean virtue of exactness (*akribeia*), and at the political climax of his story (233) he alludes to that sombre historian's most sombre scene, the 'Melian dialogue'. The Praetorians, like imperial Athens, imposed their will by naked force.

That, in the end, is the message of his narrative. Perhaps some of his readers did take it as he said he intended, as a lesson on the providence of God. But I imagine there were more who read it as we read it today, as a story of wasted heroism and the triumph of armed force. Chaerea's idealism, and the restoration of republican government that it brought about, had no chance against the Praetorians and their puppet emperor.

The old Republic was *SPQR*, the Senate and People of Rome. Tacitus pointedly adjusted the old formula to express the nature of the Principate: now it was 'the Senate, the People, and the soldiers'.[29] What Josephus has preserved for us is an authentic, contemporary Roman view, a generation earlier than Tacitus, of the events that brought about the change.

Notes

1   Suet. *Tiberius* 25.1. Retirement: *ibid.* 24.2, Tac. *Ann.* IV 9.1.
2   Suet. *Cal.* 11.
3   Suet. *Cal.* 29.1.
4   J. *Life* 1–2. For excellent recent accounts of Josephus' life and writings, see Rajak, Bilde and Sterling 226–310; also E. Schürer, *The History of the Jewish People in the Age of Jesus Christ* (rev. ed. Edinburgh 1973) 143–63.
5   See Rajak ch. 2.
6   *Life* 13–16; Rajak 39–45.

7 Details in Rajak ch. 6, Bilde 43–52. See Raphael for a brilliantly imagined analysis of his motives.

8 J. *Bell.* III 352 (trans. G.A. Williamson).

9 *Bell.* V 392; Bilde 55–7.

10 *Bell.* I 6; Rajak ch. 7.

11 *Life* 423.

12 *Life* 261–3; Jones 113–14 for the date.

13 See Edmondson et al.

14 Tac. *Hist.* II 101 (cf. *Hist.* I 1, *Ann.* I 1.2).

15 Pliny *Letters* IX 19.5; Tac. *Hist.* IV 43, *Ann.* XIII 20.2, XIV 2.2; see Appendix 2 below.

16 Quintilian X 1.104; Tac. *Agr.* 10.3, *Ann.* XIII 20.2, XIV 2.2, XV 61.3.

17 Pliny *NH* praef. 20; Pliny *Letters* III 5.6; Tac. *Ann.* XIII 20.2, XV 53.4, cf. XIII 31. For all three writers, see Syme *Tac.* 178–80, 287–94, 675.

18 For other recent analyses see Schwartz 23–30, Galimberti 39–55, and the articles of Goud and Scherberich.

19 For possible evidence of Josephus' editorial work, see the commentary on 27 and 190, and Scherberich 145–8.

20 See the commentary on 17, 216, 219. That identification might explain the interest in *equites* at section 3.

21 See 12–14, 261 (*doulokratia*); 224, 228, 236, 250, 255, 260 (Senate); also 158 and 228 on popular loyalty to Gaius.

22 See the commentary on 92. Syme *Tac.* 287f, and in *Ten Studies in Tacitus* (Oxford 1970) 105.

23 Timpe *RG* 490–2, 497. (Servilius' obituary: Tac. *Ann.* XIV 19.)

24 See the commentary on 81, 129, 130, 184.

25 See the commentary on 123, 125, 148, 154, 159, 185, 191.

26 See the commentary on 130, 202, 214, 270.

27 E.g. at 3, 4, 24, 75, 158, 202, 223.

28 See the commentary on 49, 72, 83, 90, 130, 141, 172, 178, 181, 223, 233, 241.

29 'Senatus milesque et populus' (*Ann.* I 7.2), 'populus et senatus et miles' (*Ann.* XI 30.2), 'militi patribusque et plebi' (*Ann.* XIV 11.1), 'patres aut populum aut urbanum militem' (*Hist.* I 4).

Abbreviations and Select Bibliography

Balsdon J.P.V.D. Balsdon, *The Emperor Gaius (Caligula)*, Oxford 1934.

Barrett Anthony A. Barrett, *Caligula: the Corruption of Power*, London 1989.

Bilde Per Bilde, *Flavius Josephus between Jerusalem and Rome: his Life, his Works, and their Importance* (Journal for the Study of the Pseudepigrapha, Supplement Series 2), Sheffield 1988.

Birley A.R. Birley, 'Two Unidentified Senators in Josephus, *A.J.* 19', *Classical Quarterly* 50 (2000) 620–3.

Charlesworth M.P. Charlesworth, 'The Tradition about Caligula', *Cambridge Historical Journal* 4 (1933) 105–19.

Dio Cassius Dio, *Roman History*, c. AD 207–19. English translation in Loeb Classical Library.

Edmondson et al. Jonathan Edmondson, Steve Mason and James Rives (eds), *Flavius Josephus and Flavian Rome*, Oxford 2005.

Feldman Louis H. Feldman, ed. and trans., *Josephus, Jewish Antiquities Books XVIII–XIX* (Loeb Classical Library, Josephus vol. 9), London 1965.

Ferrill Arther Ferrill, *Caligula: Emperor of Rome*, London 1991.

Galimberti Alessandro Galimberti, *I Giulio-Claudi in Flavio Giuseppe (AI XVIII–XX)* (Studi di Storia greca e romana 3), Alessandria 2001.

Goud Thomas E. Goud, 'The Sources of Josephus *Antiquities* 19', *Historia* 45 (1996) 472–82.

J. Ant. Flavius Josephus, *Antiquitates Iudaicae*, c. AD 81–94. English translation in Loeb Classical Library.

J. Bell. Flavius Josephus, *Bellum Iudaicum*, c. AD 72–81. English translation in Penguin Classics (*The Jewish War*).

J. *Life*.   Flavius Josephus, *Vita,* c. AD 94. English translation in Loeb
                   Classical Library (Josephus vol. 1).

Jones   Christopher P. Jones, 'Towards a Chronology of Josephus',
                   Scripta Classica Israelica 21 (2002) 113–21.

Jung   Helmut Jung, 'Der Thronerhebung des Claudius', *Chiron* 2
                   (1972) 367–86.

Levick   Barbara Levick, *Claudius,* London 1990.

Millar   Fergus Millar, *The Emperor in the Roman World,* London 1977.

Momigliano   Arnaldo Momigliano, 'Osservazioni sulle fonti per la storia
                   di Caligola, Claudio, Nerone', in *Quinto contributo alla storia
                   degli studi classici e del mondo antico* (Rome 1975) 799–836.

Noè   Eralda Noè, *Storiografia imperiale pretacitiana: linee di
                   svolgimento* (Pubblicazioni della Facoltà di Lettere e Filosofia
                   dell'Università di Pavia 34), Florence 1984.

Philo *Leg*.   Philo of Alexandria, *Legatio ad Gaium,* c. AD 45. English
                   translation in Loeb Classical Library.

Pliny *NH*   C. Plinius Secundus (the elder Pliny), *Natural History,*
                   c. AD 70–77. English translation in Loeb Classical Library.

Rajak   Tessa Rajak, *Josephus: the Historian and his Society,* London
                   1983.

Raphael   Frederic Raphael, *A Jew Among Romans: The Life and Legacy
                   of Flavius Josephus,* New York 2013.

Ritter   H.W. Ritter, 'Cluvius Rufus bei Josephus? Bemerkungen zu Ios.
                   Ant. 19, 91f', *Rheinisches Museum* 115 (1972) 85–91.

Scherberich   Klaus Scherberich, 'Josephus und seine Quellen im 19 Buch
                   der Antiquitates Iudaicae (Ant. Iud. 19, 1–273)', *Klio* 83 (2001)
                   134–51.

Schwartz   Daniel R. Schwartz, *Agrippa I: The Last King of Judaea* (Texte
                   und Studien zum antiken Judentum 23), Tübingen 1990.

Sen. *Const*. L. Annaeus Seneca, *De constantia sapientis,* c. AD 50. English
                   translation in Loeb Classical Library (Seneca *Moral Essays*
                   vol. 1).

Smallwood   E. Mary Smallwood, ed., *Documents Illustrating the Principates
                   of Gaius Claudius and Nero,* Cambridge 1967.

Sterling   Gregory E. Sterling, *Historiography and Self-Definition:
                   Josephos, Luke-Acts and Apologetic Historiography* (Novum
                   Testamentum Supplement 64), Leiden 1992.

Suet. *Cal.*	Suetonius Tranquillus, *De vita Caesarum*, c. AD 125:
Suet. *Claud.*	*C. Caligula* and *Divus Claudius*. English translation in Penguin Classics (*The Twelve Caesars*).
Swan	Michael Swan, 'Josephus, *A.J.*, XIX, 251–52: Opposition to Gaius and Claudius', *American Journal of Philology* 91 (1970) 149–64.
Syme *AA*	Ronald Syme, *The Augustan Aristocracy*, Oxford 1986.
Syme *Tac.*	Ronald Syme, *Tacitus*, Oxford 1958.
Tac. *Agr.*	Cornelius Tacitus, *De vita Agricolae*, c. AD 97. English translation in Penguin Classics (*Agricola and Germania*).
Tac. *Ann.*	Cornelius Tacitus, Annals, c. AD 110–20. English translation by A.J. Woodman (Indianapolis 2004).
Tac. *Hist.*	Cornelius Tacitus, Historiae, c. AD 100–10. English translation in Penguin Classics (*The Histories*).
Talbert	Richard J.A. Talbert, *The Senate of Imperial Rome*, Princeton 1984.
Timpe *RG*	Dieter Timpe, 'Römische Geschichte bei Flavius Josephus', *Historia* 9 (1960) 474–502.
Timpe *UK*	Dieter Timpe, *Untersuchungen zur Kontinuität des frühen Prinzipats* (Historia Einzelschrift 5), Wiesbaden 1962.
Vict. *Caes.*	Sex. Aurelius Victor, *De Caesaribus*, AD 358–60.
Wirszubski	Ch. Wirszubski, *Libertas as a Political Idea at Rome during the Late Republic and Early Principate*, Cambridge 1950.
Wiseman *KC*	T.P. Wiseman, 'Killing Caligula', in *Talking to Virgil: a Miscellany* (Exeter 1992) 1–13.
Wiseman *Pal.*	T.P. Wiseman, 'The Palatine, from Evander to Elagabalus', *Journal of Roman Studies* 103 (2013) 234–68.

Flavius Josephus

Antiquitates Iudaicae XIX 1–273

I

Preface

1   It was not only the Jews in Jerusalem and Judaea who were exposed to Gaius' outrageous madness. He projected it through every land and sea, and filled Rome's dominions with more evil than 2 history had ever known. But Rome above all felt the horror of his actions.

  He felt no special respect for the capital, but persecuted the Senate in particular, and those of its number who were of noble birth or 3 honoured for their ancestors' distinction. Against the 'knights', too, his ingenuity was boundless. Their dignity and financial influence made them equal to the senatorial order in the city's regard, since the senators were chosen from their number. They now faced dishonour, exile, death and plundered property—for the removal of their riches was usually his motive for their murder.

4   He was also in the process of making himself a god. The honours he demanded from his subjects were no longer those appropriate to a human being. When he visited the temple of Jupiter, which the Romans call the Capitol and regard as their most venerable temple, 5 he boldly addressed the god as his brother. Equally insane was what he did with the crossing from Dikaiarchia to Misenum (two coastal towns in Campania). Thinking it intolerable to go across by 6 warship, especially since he was lord of the sea, which owed him just as much tribute as the land did, he joined the two promontories together across three miles of water, cut off the whole bay, and drove his chariot across the bridge. That, he said, was the sort of road-building appropriate to a god.

7   He plundered every temple in Greece, giving orders that all their paintings and sculptures, statues and dedications, should be brought to him, since it was right that beautiful objects should only be in the most beautiful place, and that happened to be the city of

8 Rome. With this loot he decorated his house and gardens, and all his villas throughout Italy.

He did not even hesitate to order the transfer to Rome of Pheidias' statue of Olympian Zeus (so called because it is venerated by the Greeks at Olympia), and the only reason he failed to carry

9 it out was that the architects told Memmius Regulus that to move the statue, as he had been ordered, would totally ruin it. It is said that Memmius postponed the operation both for this reason and because portents occurred that were too significant for anyone

10 to disbelieve; he reported them to Gaius at the risk of his life, to explain why he had failed to act on the emperor's instruction, and he only survived because Gaius died first.

11 His madness even extended to carrying his new-born daughter to the Capitol and placing her on the knees of Jupiter's statue. She had two fathers, he said, and belonged both to him and to Jupiter; which of the two was the greater he left undecided.

12 People put up with even that. But he also incited the slaves to bring accusations against their masters on any charges they liked; whatever they might say was dangerous in that most of the complaints were

13 made to please him, and at his suggestion. Polydeuces, slave of Claudius, was encouraged to bring such an accusation straight away, and Gaius was even present in court to hear a capital charge made against his own uncle. (He was hoping to be given the chance of doing away with him, but that was not how it turned out.)

14 When he had now filled the whole world—his own realm—with miseries and false accusations, raising up slaves to rule their own masters, many plots were made against him. Some who conspired did so in anger, to avenge what they had suffered; others undertook to deal with the man before they fell into disaster themselves.

15 His death was a great turning-point in human happiness, for the laws and security of all men and particularly for our own nation, which only just escaped total ruin thanks to his sudden end. I

16 therefore intend to give an exact account of the whole story, not least because it offers a weighty proof of the power of God. It also provides reassurance for those in affliction, and a lesson in prudence for those who think that good fortune lasts for ever, and do not realise that unaccompanied by righteousness it will bring them to misery.

II

The Conspiracy

17 Three ways to death were being prepared for Gaius, each of them under the leadership of a good man. One group gathered around Aemilius Regulus, a native of Cordoba in Spain, who was eager that either he or his companions should do away with him. Another

18 group being organised to help them was led by Cassius Chaerea, a military tribune. Last but not least, Annius Minucianus was also among those preparing to attack the tyranny.

19 They all had their reasons to detest Gaius and conspire against him. Regulus was angry with the whole situation; he hated unjust deeds with the hot temper of a free man, even to the extent of not wanting his plans kept secret. (At any rate, he shared them with many of his friends, and with others whom he considered men

20 of action.) Minucianus' motive in the undertaking was partly to avenge his close friend Lepidus, a man with few equals in Rome whom Gaius had killed, and partly because he was himself afraid

21 of Gaius, whose murderous anger was let loose on all alike. As for Chaerea, he was humiliated by Gaius' insulting allegations of effeminacy; and because he was on close terms with Gaius and in his service, he was in any case in daily danger. It would be less servile, he thought, to put an end to him.

22 By common consent they laid out the matter for consideration to all those who were witnesses of the outrages and were eager to avoid the crisis afflicting others by getting rid of Gaius. Perhaps they would succeed; and if they did, with such great benefits at stake, even if their labours achieved the goal at the cost of their own destruction, it would be a happy outcome for the safety of the city

23 and the empire. Chaerea above all was urging action. He longed to enhance his reputation; and besides, since it was easier for an officer to approach Gaius, he would have the opportunity to kill him.

24 Meanwhile, the chariot races were on. The Romans are fanatically keen on this type of show and eagerly assemble in the Circus Maximus to watch it. The crowds there petition emperors for what they want, and emperors who decide not to resist their requests are
25 particularly popular. On this occasion they were asking Gaius with heartfelt entreaties to lighten their burden a little by remitting taxes. But he would not listen, and when they shouted louder he sent men out into various parts of the crowd with orders to arrest all those
26 shouting, drag them out and execute them on the spot. He gave the order, the men carried it out, and many people were killed as a result. So the people submitted and stopped shouting; they could see with their own eyes that begging for benefits on those terms brought them instant death.

27 This made Chaerea more determined to get his plan under way, and to put an end to Gaius' brutal way of treating people. Several times at the games he was on the point of making an attempt but calculation made him hold back. Not that he now had any doubts about the killing; but he was looking for the ideal moment, so that when he struck it would fulfil his plans, not waste them.

28 As a long-serving soldier, Chaerea did not enjoy his intimacy with Gaius. When Gaius put him in charge of enforcing payment of taxes and other debts to the emperor's treasury, which were overdue because the rate had been doubled, Chaerea took his time over the exactions, acting in his own way and not as Gaius had
29 ordered. Angry at this merciful and considerate attitude towards the taxpayers, Gaius blamed him for the slow collection of the money, and accused him of being spineless.

He insulted Chaerea in other ways too. Whenever it was Chaerea's day on duty and he asked for the password, Gaius would give him some humiliating word appropriate to a woman.
30 He did this even though he himself was not free from the imputation. For in the rites of a certain mystery-cult, which he had set up himself, Gaius used to put on women's clothes, and invent wigs and other disguises for making himself look female. But that did not stop him attaching the same stigma to Chaerea.
31 Chaerea was furious each time he received the password, and even more so when he passed it on and was laughed at by his

colleagues. The other officers joined in the game at his expense, discussing in advance, when it was his turn to bring them Caesar's password, which of the usual amusing words he would come back with.

32   So Chaerea, with these good reasons to be angry, was confident enough to bring others into partnership with him.

There was a certain Pompedius, a man of senatorial rank who had held almost all the magistracies, but who otherwise led the

33   inactive life of an Epicurean. He was accused by his enemy Timidius of having uttered disgraceful slanders against Gaius. As witness, Timidius called Quintilia, a stage performer whose youth and

34   beauty gave her many admirers, including Pompedius. The charge was false, and the girl refused to give evidence that would send her lover to his death. Timidius demanded torture. Gaius, in a fury, told Chaerea not to waste time but to put her to the torture straight away. He used Chaerea for murder trials and others where torture was needed, reckoning that he would do the job more brutally to avoid the slur of being feeble.

35   As Quintilia was being taken to the torture, she trod on the foot of one of those involved, as a sign to be brave and not fear for her interrogation; she would bear it with the courage of a man. Chaerea, unwillingly but under compulsion, submitted her to cruel torture; she did not give in, and he brought her back into Gaius' presence in

36   a state that would give no pleasure to her audience. Even Gaius felt some compunction at the sight of Quintilia's dreadful condition after her ordeal. He acquitted both her and Pompedius, and honoured her with a gift of money; it was to console her for the mutilation that had ruined her beauty, and for her unbearable agonies.

37   Chaerea was in desperate distress; he had done his best to cause harm to people whom even Gaius thought worthy of consolation. So he went and talked to Clemens the commander of the Guard, and to Papinius, who like himself was a military tribune.

38   'Well, Clemens,' he said, 'as the emperor's *guards*, we have carried out our duties very thoroughly indeed. By our vigilance and hard work, we have killed some of those who conspired against him and tortured others until even he was sorry for them. That's real bravery in the exercise of military duty!'

39 Clemens said nothing. He flushed, and gave Chaerea a glance that showed he was ashamed of the orders he had to carry out, even though for his own safety he was not prepared to speak openly to

40 them of the emperor's madness. Encouraged, and speaking now without fear of danger, Chaerea enlarged on the horrors that kept the city and the empire in thrall.

41 'In theory Gaius is the man responsible for it all. But Clemens, if you look at the facts, it is I myself, and Papinius here, and you more than either of us, who are applying these tortures to the Romans and to all the human race. It's not because we obey Gaius' orders;

42 since it is in our power to stop him acting so outrageously against citizens and subject peoples, the fact that we obey him is our own choice.

'We aren't soldiers—we're bodyguards and public executioners! We bear these arms not to defend the freedom and sovereignty of the Romans, but to protect the man who has enslaved their bodies and their minds! Every day we kill them and torture them, polluting ourselves with blood until the time when someone else at Gaius' bidding will do the same to us!

43 'The fact that we do these things doesn't make him friendly towards us. On the contrary, he suspects us all the more as the tally of deaths has increased. He will never put a stop to his fury, since the object of it is not justice but his own pleasure; and we too are going to be set up as targets. Our duty is to secure the safety and freedom of the public—and to resolve to get out of danger ourselves.'

44 Clemens did not conceal his approval of Chaerea's intention. But he told him to keep quiet: if the word reached too many ears, and what should be kept secret was allowed to leak out, the plot would be discovered and they would be punished before they had a chance to act. 'Your chance will come,' he said; 'leave it to time and the

45 hope time brings. As for me, I'm too old for this sort of venture. Perhaps I could suggest a safer policy than the one you speak of, but no-one could propose a more honourable one.'

46 Clemens went home, thinking hard about what he had heard, and what he had said himself. Chaerea was anxious. He hurried to Cornelius Sabinus, a fellow-tribune whom he knew to be an

47 excellent man—a lover of liberty and therefore hostile to the present state of things. Chaerea wanted to get the plan quickly under way, and thought it good to have Sabinus as an ally. He was afraid that Clemens might talk; and in any case, delaying and putting off the moment seemed appropriate only to procrastinators.

48 Sabinus welcomed the whole plan. He had come to just the same conclusion himself, but had not known whom it would be safe to talk to about it and had therefore kept silent. Now he had found a man who not only agreed to keep what he heard secret, but even revealed his own plans to him. Much excited, Sabinus begged Chaerea to waste no time.

49 They turned to Minucianus, who was congenial to them in excellence of character and devotion to noble ideals. Gaius, however, viewed him with suspicion as a result of the death of Lepidus, since Lepidus and Minucianus had been very close friends. So he too was

50 in fear for his life. Gaius was a source of terror to all senior senators, never relaxing his rage against them individually and collectively.

51 They understood each other's unhappiness at the state of affairs, and though for fear of danger they did not openly speak their mind about how they hated Gaius, they knew it in other ways and thus stayed on good terms with one another.

52 When they met, the proper respects were paid; as on previous occasions, Chaerea and Sabinus deferred to Minucianus' preeminence, his high nobility of birth, and the general excellence

53 of his reputation. To get the conversation started, Minucianus took the initiative and asked Chaerea what password he had been given that day. For the insults Chaerea suffered in the passwords affair were the talk of the town.

54 Chaerea was glad he had asked and immediately returned the confidence Minucianus had shown in discussing the matter in such terms.

'Liberty,' he said, 'is the password *you* give me! Thank you for

55 urging me even more than I urge myself: if you agree with us, and we have been of one mind even before this meeting, then 1 need no further words of encouragement.

56 'One sword in my belt will be enough for us both—so let us get to work! Either you be our leader, and give me orders to go wherever

you think fit, or I shall go first myself in the confidence of your support and collaboration.

57 　'Those who have the heart for action will not be short of weapons—it's always the heart that makes weapons work. I am eager for this enterprise, and what may happen to me personally is of no significance. There's no time to think about my own danger. What causes me anguish is the enslavement of our country, once the freest in the world; the authority of the laws has been taken away, and thanks to Gaius all men face destruction.

58 　'You are the judge; since we are agreed and you have not abandoned us, let me be worthy of your trust in such a cause!'

59 　Recognising the urgency of Chaerea's words, Minucianus gladly embraced him. He added further encouragement and praise of his daring, embraced him again, and sent him on his way with heartfelt prayers.

60 　There are some who insist that those prayers were heard. They say that when Chaerea was entering the Senate-house a voice was heard from the crowd urging him on and telling him to do what had to

61 　be done with the help of divine power. At first Chaerea thought he had been discovered and that one of the conspirators had betrayed him. Then he realised that it was the first encouragement—either one of the conspirators giving a signal to urge him on or even the very voice of God raising his courage. For God does watch over the deeds of men.

62 　The plot had now reached many people. All of them—senators, knights, and those of the soldiers who knew about it—were ready and armed, since no-one was in any doubt that the removal of Gaius

63 　would be a blessing. For that reason all of them in their different ways were eager not to fall short, if they could help it, of the courage needed for such a task. With the utmost resolution and effort, both in word and in action, they were keyed up to kill a tyrant.

64 　That was true even of Callistus. He was a freedman of Gaius, and this one man more than any other had reached a position of great power under him. His power indeed was nothing short of despotic, thanks to his vast wealth and the fact that everyone was afraid of

65 　him. In bribe-taking, arrogance and abuse of power he was without equal. Callistus knew very well how innately ruthless Gaius was

and how he could never be swayed from what he had decided on. He knew too that there were many sources of danger to himself, not least his huge fortune. So he even paid court to Claudius, and shifted his allegiance secretly to him.

66

Callistus hoped that if Gaius were removed Claudius might come to power. In that case, he could secure a basis of prestige and power on the same terms by investing an advance account of gratitude and goodwill. At any rate, he boldly claimed that he had been ordered to deal with Claudius by poisoning him, but had kept on finding ways of putting off the deed.

67

I think he invented this story in order to secure Claudius' favour. If Gaius had been determined to deal with Claudius, he would not have put up with any excuses from Callistus; if Callistus had been ordered to do it, he would not have found it a duty to be avoided; and if Callistus had disobeyed his master's orders, he would have paid the price straight away. No, it was some heavenly power that enabled Claudius to escape the madness of Gaius, and Callistus' claim on his gratitude was merely a baseless pretence.

68

69

III

The Assassination

70   Chaerea's companions caused daily postponements. Many of them were hesitant, unlike Chaerea himself, who would not willingly delay action but thought any moment appropriate for the deed.

71   Opportunities were frequent when Gaius went up to the Capitol for the sacrifices offered on behalf of his daughter. When he stood on top of the basilica, throwing gold and silver coins to the people, he could have been hurled down headlong from the high roof overlooking the forum. Or during the performance of the mystery-

72   cult he had established—for in his determination to conduct himself properly, he was oblivious to everything, and confidently refused to believe that anyone would attack him. Even if there came no sign

73   from heaven to give Chaerea the power of execution, he had enough bodily strength himself to despatch Gaius then, even without a sword.

  So Chaerea was furious with his colleagues, fearing that the

74   opportunities would slip through their fingers. But though they could see he had legality on his side, and was urging them for their own good, they still thought he should postpone it, at least for a little while. They were afraid that if the attempt somehow went wrong, there would be chaos in the city as those who had knowledge of the plot were hunted down, and the next would-be assassins would find their valour useless because Gaius would be more on his guard against them.

75   So they decided that the best time to make the attempt was while the Palatine Games were on. These shows are held in honour of the Caesar who first transferred power from the Republic to himself. There is a wooden hut just in front of the imperial residence, and the audience, besides the emperor, consists of the Roman nobility with their wives and children.

76   It would be easy for them to make their attempt as he entered; with so many thousands of people crowded in a narrow space, his guards would not have the chance to help him even if any of them wanted to.

77   Chaerea consented to this, and it was agreed to act on the first day of the Games. But their plan could not compete with fortuitous delays. Even though three days were added to the scheduled programme, they were hard put to it to get their business done on the last.

78   Chaerea called a meeting. 'All this time wasted,' he said, 'puts to shame our delay in carrying out what we planned so bravely. And it is dangerous: if we are informed against, the plan will fail and

79 Gaius will be still more savage. Can't we see that every extra day we allow to Gaius' tyranny is one day less for freedom? From now on we have to be fearless. The happiness of others is in our hands. We must make ourselves, for all time, the object of posterity's honour and admiration.'

80   Unable either to deny the truth of his words or to undertake the deed at once, they kept a strained silence.

    'Gentlemen!' said Chaerea. 'Why do we hesitate? Don't you realise that today is the last day of the Games, and Gaius is about

81 to set sail?' (He had made arrangements to sail to Alexandria, on a visit to Egypt.) 'A fine thing, to let him slip from our hands and go parading across land and sea, disgracing Rome's imperial pride!

82 Suppose some Egyptian found his insolence more than freeborn men could stand, and killed him—what would we think of ourselves if *that* humiliation happened?

83   'Well, I have had enough of your excuses. I shall face the danger now, today, and gladly bear whatever it may bring. I would not postpone it even if I could. Shall someone else kill Gaius while I live, and rob me of the honour of his death? What could be worse for a man with any pride?'

84   Chaerea was as good as his word. He set about the task himself, and gave courage to the others. All were eager to get on with it without further delay.

85   At dawn Chaerea hurried to the Palatine. He was wearing the cavalry sword which is the proper equipment for military tribunes

86   when asking the emperor for the password. (It was Chaerea's turn to receive the password that day.) There was already a noisy, jostling crowd converging on the Palatine to get their places early for the show. Gaius liked popular enthusiasm at such events, and had therefore not set aside any special places for the senate or the knights. So the seating was indiscriminate, women next to men, slaves next to free.

87   Arriving in procession, Gaius sacrificed to Augustus Caesar, in whose honour the whole show was being held. As one of the sacrificial animals was killed, it happened that a senator called Asprenas had his toga stained with blood. That made Gaius laugh, but for Asprenas it was a clear omen (he was, in fact, butchered

88   immediately after Gaius). That day, so it is said, Gaius was full of uncharacteristic affability; everyone present was astonished at the good humour of his conversation.

89
90   After the sacrifice, Gaius turned to the show and took his seat, with the most prominent of his friends around him. The theatre was a wooden structure, put up every year in the following way. It had two doors, one leading into the open, one into a portico for people to go in and out without disturbing those segregated inside, and within from the hut itself, which separated off another room by partitions as a retreat for competitors and performers of all kinds.

91   The audience settled down. The emperor occupied the right-hand extremity of the theatre; Chaerea and the other tribunes were not far away. Bathybius, a senator of praetorian rank, was sitting next to Cluvius, an ex-consul. Taking care not to be overheard, he asked

92   him whether any news of revolution had come to his ears. Cluvius replied that he had heard nothing. 'Well, Cluvius, today's contest is a tyrannicide.' To which Cluvius answered, 'Friend, hold thy peace, lest other of the Greeks should hear thy word.'

93   Gaius, meanwhile, was amusing himself. He had quantities of fruit tipped on to the spectators, and also birds rare enough to be valuable to those who got them; he then watched the fights that broke out as the audience snatched and scrambled for them.

94   Two omens, I notice, also took place at that time. The mime on the programme was one in which a leader is caught and crucified,

and the play presented by the dancer was *Cinyras,* in which Cinyras himself and his daughter Myrrha are both killed; so there was a great deal of artificial blood poured out, first around the man on the cross and then around Cinyras. Moreover, it is agreed that the date was that on which Philip son of Amyntas, king of Macedon, was killed by Pausanias, one of his companions, as he was entering the theatre.

95

96 Gaius was wondering whether to go and bathe, have lunch and then come back, as he had done before, or to stay to the end of the programme, since it was the last day. Minucianus, sitting behind him, was afraid that their opportunities might dissolve into nothing when he saw that Chaerea had already gone out. He got up in haste

97 to get to Chaerea and urge him to be bold. Gaius, all amiability, caught at his toga. 'Where are you off, my dear fellow?' he said. Minucianus sat down, to show courtesy to the emperor (though fear was the stronger motive). He stayed only a moment before getting

98 up again. This time Gaius did not stop him, thinking that he was leaving for some necessary purpose. Meanwhile Asprenas, who also wanted to bring the plot to a conclusion, was urging Gaius to do what he had done before—slip away for a bath and lunch and then come back in.

99 Chaerea and his team were keeping each other posted as opportunity offered. Whatever the effort, each man had to stand at his allotted position and not leave it; but it was now mid-afternoon, and the passage of time and postponement of action were agonising.

100 Gaius' lateness made Chaerea resolve to go back inside and attack him in his seat. He could see that this would result in great bloodshed among the senators and those of the knights who were nearby, but that fear did not lessen his determination; he thought it right to regard the fate of the casualties a small price to pay for the security and liberty of all.

101 The conspirators had actually turned to go into the theatre when the hubbub told them that Gaius had risen to leave. So they turned back and thrust the crowd out of the way, supposedly to prevent annoyance to Gaius, but in fact to make things safer for themselves. They wanted to get Gaius away from any helpers before they set about the killing.

102 The first to come out were Gaius' uncle Claudius, his brother-in-law Marcus Vinicius, and Valerius Asiaticus. The conspirators would have liked to block their way, but respect for their dignity made it impossible. Then came the emperor with Paullus Arruntius.

103 When he was inside the residence, he left the direct routes along which the slaves attending on him were standing, and which
104 Claudius and the others had taken, and turned down an empty alleyway as a short-cut. He was intending to go to the baths, and also to inspect the boys from Asia, who had come in solemn procession to sing at the mysteries he was celebrating (and some of them also to perform in Pyrrhic dances at the theatres).

105 Chaerea presented himself and asked for the password. When Gaius gave one of his mocking words, Chaerea did not hesitate. With a curse, he drew his sword and struck a savage blow. But it was not fatal.

106 I know there are some who say that Chaerea deliberately did not finish Gaius off with one blow, wanting to exact a greater vengeance
107 by wounding him many times. But I cannot believe this version: in such actions fear does not allow calculation. If Chaerea did intend that, then I think he was utterly foolish to indulge his passion rather than acting quickly to get himself and his comrades out of danger. There were many ways for help to reach Gaius while he was still breathing—and then Chaerea would have been concerned with vengeance not on Gaius but on himself and his friends. Even if the
108 deed were done, it would be better to do it in silence and escape the anger of the guards; when success was still uncertain, he was hardly likely to act senselessly and lose both the opportunity and his life. However, anyone who wants to can make whatever guesses he likes on this matter.

109 Gaius was disoriented by the pain of the blow. The sword had struck him between neck and shoulder, but the collarbone stopped it from going any further. He did not shout in terror, or call for any of his friends; either he didn't trust them or he couldn't think anyway. Groaning in the extremity of his pain, he ran forward to
110 escape. But Cornelius Sabinus had already anticipated his intention.

Sabinus caught Gaius and pushed him over his knee. Several of them stood round him as he lay there, and at a single word hacked at him with their swords, urging each other on and even competing with each other in the deed.

In the end, it was Aquila who dealt the blow that finished him off.
111 That is agreed by everybody without dispute. But Chaerea should have the credit for the deed, even though he had many collabo-rators. He first worked out how it could be done, and set about it
112 long before all of them. He first had the courage to speak out to the others, and gathered together the various individuals who accepted the assassination plan. His intelligence put it all together, and the plans he suggested put him far above the rest. It was his good speeches that won them over when their nerve failed and forced
113 them all to go on. And it is clear that when the moment came for action the initiative was his: he seized the honour of the killing and left Gaius a doomed man, an easy victim for the rest. In all justice, therefore, whatever the others did should be credited to Chaerea's intelligence and valour, and the labour of his hands.

IV

Panic on the Palatine

114 Such was the end of Gaius, lying lifeless from his many wounds.
115 Now that they had finished with him, Chaerea and his friends saw
     that there was no escape if they went back the same way. What
     caused them hesitation was the act itself; for great danger faced
     the assassins of an emperor whom the foolish people loved and
     honoured, and when the soldiers came to look for him there would
116 be bloodshed. Besides, the streets were narrow where they had done
     the deed, and blocked by a great crowd—not only the servants, but
     also the soldiers who were on duty that day to guard the emperor.
117 So they went by different streets, and reached the house of
     Germanicus, father of Gaius whom they had just killed, which
     was adjacent. (This was because the imperial residence, though a
     unity, was made up severally of the buildings belonging to each
     one of those who had been born in the ruling power, named after
     those who had built them or even begun building any of the parts.)
118 Having got away from the approach of the crowd, they were safe
     for the moment while no-one yet knew what disaster had befallen
     the emperor.
119 The first people to realise that Gaius was dead were his German
     bodyguard, who made up the unit named after the Celtic nation
120 from which they were recruited. Their national characteristic is
     hot temper of a kind rare even among other barbarians, since the
     Germans are less able to calculate their actions. Physically very
     powerful, they achieve great results by engaging at the first rush
121 any whom they decide are enemies. Their judgements are based on
     their own advantage, not the general merits of the case, and Gaius
     had secured their goodwill with gifts of money. So they loved him,
     and when they heard of his murder they felt it deeply.

122   Sabinus was in charge of them—an officer whose command over such men was due to physical strength rather than the excellence and nobility of his ancestors; he was, in fact, a gladiator. With drawn swords, the Germans went through the house in search of Caesar's murderers.

123   They butchered Asprenas, because he was the first person they met. He was the man mentioned above, whose bloodstained toga at the sacrifice was an evil omen for his fate.

    The second to run into them was Norbanus Balbus. Though he was one of the noblest of Roman citizens, with many generals among his ancestors, they paid no respect to his rank. But he was

124 very strong; as they attacked, he grappled with the first of them and wrenched away his sword, showing that he was not going to be killed without a fight. Eventually, however, surrounded by many assailants, he fell beneath a hail of blows.

125   The third was Anteius, a leading senator. Unlike the others, he did not meet the Germans by chance. He wanted to be a spectator, to enjoy in person the sight of Gaius lying there, and indulge his hatred of him. For Gaius had driven his father, the elder Anteius, into exile, and not content with that, had sent soldiers to kill him.

126 That was the reason Anteius was there, rejoicing as he looked at the corpse; but when the hubbub began in the house and he realised he had to hide, he could not avoid the thoroughness of the Germans' search and their murderous savagery against guilty and innocent alike.

127   So these men died. In the theatre, meanwhile, there was horror and disbelief when the word came that Gaius was dead. Those to whom the news of his death would be sheer pleasure, who would have reckoned it one of the best things that could happen to them,

128 were too afraid to believe it. Those on the other hand who, far from
129 hoping, did not want any such thing to happen to Gaius—women and children, all the slaves, some of the soldiers—were reluctant to accept the truth on the grounds that no human being could be brave enough to do it.

    The reason for the soldiers' attitude was the pay they received and the fact that they were, in effect, partners in Gaius' tyranny; as the ministers of his outrageous behaviour, and the weapon

130   he employed to terrorise the leading citizens, they gained both
profit and respect. The women and the younger generation had
been won over by popular delights—games, gladiatorial shows,
and the enjoyment of certain meat-distributions which were in
theory for the welfare of the people but in fact to satisfy Gaius'

131   bloodthirsty madness. As for the slaves, they were on familiar terms
with their masters and despised them; Gaius' aid offered them a
refuge against ill-treatment, since it was easy for them to give false
information against their masters, and be believed. They could gain
both freedom and wealth if they revealed their masters' financial
situation, since the reward for informers was one eighth of the
property of the accused.

132   If any of the aristocrats believed the story, whether because they
wanted to or because they knew in advance about the plot, they kept
silent, concealing both their joy at the news and even the fact that

133   they had heard it. Those who wanted to believe it were afraid that if
their hopes proved false they would be punished for revealing their
opinions prematurely. Those who knew it was true because they
were in the plot concealed it all the more; they did not know who
their comrades were, and dared not speak to anyone who might
gain from the continuation of the tyranny in case they should be

134   denounced and punished if Gaius were alive after all. For a rival
story had got around that Gaius was wounded but not killed; he
was alive, and doctors were looking after him.

135   No-one trusted anyone enough to speak his mind with confidence
to his neighbour. He might be a friend of Gaius, suspect because
of his sympathy with the tyranny; or if he hated him, his total *lack*

136   of sympathy would make what he said quite unreliable. One story
dashed the aristocrats' joyful hopes most of all: some people were
claiming that Gaius had shrugged off the danger and escaped to
the Forum, not even bothering to have his wounds treated, and was
now, still covered in blood, haranguing the people.

137   This was guesswork, due not to reason but to the mere desire to
talk. How it was taken depended on the attitude of the hearers. But
they did not leave the safety of their seats. They were afraid of the
accusation that would be brought against whoever went out first,
since judgement would be passed not on their actual purpose in

going out, but on whatever motive the prosecutors and judges might choose to attribute to them.

138   When a mob of Germans with drawn swords surrounded the theatre, the audience all expected to die. They were terrified no matter who came in, and expected to be cut to pieces on the spot. There was no escape: they could not summon the courage to leave, but they did not believe it was safe to stay where they were.

139   As the Germans burst in, the theatre rang with cries for mercy. On their knees, the audience begged them to believe that they knew nothing at all about what had happened or about the intentions

140   of the rebels, if there really was a rebellion. 'Spare us! Don't take vengeance on the innocent for someone else's crime! Whatever has

141   been done, get a search organised for those who have done it!' This and more they cried, weeping, beating their faces, calling on the gods. Imminent danger taught them what to say, and their pleas were like those of a man on trial for his life.

142   At this the fury of the soldiers was dissipated. They changed their minds about what they were going to do to the spectators; it was brutal, and seemed so even to them in their savage mood. But they fixed the heads of Asprenas and the others on the altar.

143   That made the plight of the spectators even worse. Remembering the men's high rank and pitying their fate, they were equally terrorised themselves by the possibility of danger. It was very

144   uncertain whether in the end they would escape the same fate. So even those who hated Gaius with all their heart, and rightly, were deprived of all pleasure and joy at his death. For it was still in the balance whether they would die too; even at that point they did not yet have any good reason to believe they would survive.

145   There was an auctioneer called Arruntius Evarestus, with the powerful voice required by his profession. Possessed of wealth equal to the richest in Rome, he was able (both then and later) to do

146   whatever he wanted throughout the city. He hated Gaius as much as anyone, but the promptings of fear and the strategy needed to gain his survival were stronger than any momentary exultation.

147   So he assumed an attitude of the deepest possible grief, put on all the mourning appropriate to the death of one held in the highest honour, and proceeded to the theatre, where he formally announced

the death of Gaius. That put an end to any further ignorance about what had happened.

148　Arruntius Stella and the tribunes were already going round summoning the Germans, telling them to put away their weapons

149　and explaining to them that Gaius was dead. It is very clear that that was what saved the lives of the people packed in the theatre, and all those who in any way came into contact with the Germans. For there is nothing they would not have done if they had had any hope that the fallen Gaius had any breath left in him.

150　So excessive was their loyalty that they would even have laid down their own lives to keep him safe from attack and prevent

151　so great a misfortune happening to him. But once they knew for certain he was dead, their rage for vengeance ended; there was no point displaying zealous loyalty now that the man who would reward them was no more. Besides, they were afraid that if they continued on the rampage they would be subject to the attention of the Senate, if that was where authority would lie, or of whoever

152　else established himself in power. It was a close thing, but in the end the Germans did give up the blood-lust that had seized them at the death of Gaius.

153　Meanwhile, Chaerea was very anxious about Minucianus, in case he should fall in with the furious Germans and be killed. He went around asking each of the soldiers to take care for Minucianus' safety, and made detailed enquiries to find out that he was not dead.

154　In fact, Minucianus had been brought before Clemens, along with many other senators. Clemens let them go, agreeing with them that the deed was just and testifying to the courage of those who had conceived it and not shrunk from carrying it out.

155　'Tyranny,' he said, 'does not last long. For a while the tyrant is borne along on the pleasure of outrageous violence, but virtue hates

156　him and the end of his life cannot be happy. On the contrary, he meets an unhappy fate like that of Gaius. Long before these men rose against him and plotted their attack, Gaius had become a conspirator against himself. He was intolerable: by his outrageous behaviour, by abolishing all care for the law, he taught even his friends to make war on him. Yes, they killed Gaius, in a sense; but in reality he lies dead by his own hand.'

157   By now the security in the theatre, which had at first been so strict, was relaxed a little, and the audience got up from their seats. It was Alcyon the doctor who was responsible for their welcome release. When he was seized to look after the wounded, he sent out those who were with him—supposedly to fetch the materials needed for his treatment of the casualties, but in fact to get away from the danger they were in.

V

The Republic Restored

158   In the meantime, the Senate was in session and the people were assembled in the Forum (the customary place). Their business was to discover the murderers of Gaius, but though the people went about it eagerly, the Senate made only a pretence.

159   Valerius Asiaticus, a man of consular rank, addressed the assembly. The people were in an uproar of indignation that the emperor's murderers were still not found. 'Who did it?' they all urgently demanded of him. 'I wish I had,' he replied.

160   The consuls too put out an edict containing accusations against Gaius. They ordered the people to go home, and the soldiers to return to their quarters. In return, they promised to the people hope of seeing their grievances alleviated, and to the soldiers hope of rewards, provided they kept their accustomed discipline and did not go out on the rampage. They were afraid of serious damage to the city if the soldiers ran wild and turned to looting, or to plundering the temples.

161   By now there had already assembled the full membership of the Senate. In particular, those who had joined the plot to kill Gaius were there, full of confidence and with a high opinion of themselves, as if the government depended on them alone.

162   It was while matters were at this stage that Claudius was suddenly kidnapped from the house. The soldiers had held a meeting, and argued among themselves about what should be done. They could see that a republic would never be able to keep control of so great a state, and if it did come into being it would not govern in their interest. If on the other hand some individual should gain power it

163
164   would do them great harm not to have helped him to gain it. So the best thing was to choose an emperor themselves, while the situation was still fluid. Claudius was the man—he was the dead Gaius' uncle,

165 and more illustrious than any of those gathered in the Senate house, whether in the distinction of his ancestors or in his own devotion to learning. Besides, if they made him emperor he would probably honour them for it and reward them with handouts. That was the plan. It was carried out immediately, and Claudius was kidnapped by the soldiers.

166 Gnaeus Sentius Saturninus now addressed the Senate. He was undeterred by the news that Claudius had been taken and had made his claim to power (unwillingly, it appeared, but no doubt he really wanted it). Saturninus stood up and gave a speech of encouragement appropriate to an audience of free and honourable men. This is what he said.

167 'Romans: It seems incredible, since it comes upon us unexpectedly after so long a time, but we really do possess the dignity of freedom.

'How long it will last we do not know; that lies with the will of the gods, who have bestowed it. But it is enough to make us glad, and to
168 bring us together in joy, even if we are to be deprived of it. For men with a sense of honour and independent judgement, it is enough to live even one hour in a country that governs itself, controlled by the laws that made it great.

169 'I do not remember the old freedom; I was born too late to know it. But I am making the most of what we have now, and cannot get enough of it. Fortunate are those who were born and brought up in liberty! And worthy of no less honour than the gods themselves are these men, who have given us a taste of it—late indeed, but in our time!

170 'I pray that it may stay secure for ever; but let even this one day of it be enough for both the young and the old among us. For the older men it counts as a lifetime if they die having had experience of its blessings; for the young it is a lesson in the establishment of
171 virtue. Virtue was good for our forefathers, and now, thanks to the present moment, for us too nothing is more important than to live by it. For only virtue can devise liberty for mankind.

172 'What happened in the old days I know only from report, but I have experienced myself and seen with my own eyes the evils with which tyrannies fill the state. They discourage all excellence,

deprive generosity of its freedom, set up schools of flattery and fear—and all because they leave public affairs not to the wisdom of the laws but to the caprice of the rulers.

173   'Ever since Julius Caesar decided to destroy the Republic and throw the state into confusion by doing violence to the rule of law, making himself the master of justice but the slave of whatever brought him personal satisfaction, there is no evil that the city has

174 not suffered. And his successors in power have all vied with each other in abolishing our ancestral tradition.

  'They have done their best to leave the citizen body bereft of all nobility, thinking it safer for themselves to associate with dishonest men. As for those with a reputation for conspicuous virtue, it was not enough merely to take away a little of their pride; what was decreed was the utter destruction of all.

175   'There have been many tyrants, and grievous and intolerable rulers they have shown themselves. But one man—Gaius, who died today—outdid them all in his display of terror. His fury was indiscriminate, and he vented it not only on his fellow-citizens but even on his relatives and friends. He raged against the gods, as well as men; and the evils he inflicted went even beyond his predecessors' enthusiasm for exacting unjust revenge.

176   'For tyranny, mere pleasure is no gain; even outrageous pleasure, causing grief by assaults on property and wives, is not enough. Tyranny's full reward is the utter ruin of its enemies, root and

177 branch. All freedom is hateful to it.

  'Not even those who make light of what they have suffered can entice tyranny into goodwill; they may be magnanimous, and treat their ill fortune as beneath their notice, but the tyrant knows what evils he has inflicted on them. Unable to ignore his own deeds, he can only hope to be safe from suspicion if he is able to do away with his victims entirely.

178   'Well, now you are rid of such evils. You are accountable only to each other, which is the best of all constitutions for guaranteeing present concord, future security and the glory that goes with the prosperity of the city. It is your duty to take thought individually for the public benefit—and to declare your opinion *against* anything

179 previously suggested which you may not like. There is no danger in

that. No despot is set over you now with a free hand to ruin the city, and to remove autocratically those who open their mouths.

180
181
'What fed the tyranny was nothing other than inaction, the refusal to speak up against anything it wanted. Overcome by the pleasure of peace, we learned to live like slaves. Even those of us who suffered irremediable disaster, or saw it happen to our neighbours, were afraid of dying bravely. Death in the depths of shame was all we could expect.

182
'But our first duty is to confer the highest possible honours on the tyrannicides and on Cassius Chaerea in particular. With the gods' help, in planning and action this one man has shown himself the giver of liberty. It is right that we should remember him. In a time of tyranny, he planned our freedom and risked his life for it; in a time of freedom, we must make it our first unfettered resolution to vote him honours.

183

184
'Rewarding benefactors is an honourable act appropriate to free men, and this man has indeed proved a benefactor to us all. Cassius and Brutus, who killed Gaius Julius, do not bear comparison with him. All they did for the city was to fan the flame of political strife and civil war. But *his* tyrannicide has actually freed the city from the horrors that follow.'

185
Sentius' speech was received with pleasure by the senators and those of the knights who were present. One man, Trebellius Maximus, jumped up and snatched Sentius' ring, which had a stone set in it with an engraved portrait of Gaius. Sentius, presumably, had been so concerned with his speech and what he had to do that he had forgotten about it. The portrait was smashed.

186
The night was now well advanced, and Chaerea asked the consuls for the password. They gave him 'Liberty'. The solemn act was like a miracle that they could hardly believe. Before the city was ruled by tyrants, the consuls had been the military commanders; now, in the hundredth year since they had been robbed of the Republic, they resumed the right to give the password.

187

188
Chaerea in turn passed it on to the forces loyal to the Senate, four cohorts to whom the prospect of no emperor at all seemed more honourable than tyranny. They marched off with their tribunes.

189

The people too were now dispersing, full of joy and hope, proud that they had recovered their sovereignty and that no-one stood over them. Chaerea was everything to them.

190 Meanwhile, Chaerea himself thought it dangerous that Gaius' wife and daughter were still alive, and that his whole family had not perished with him; whatever was left of it would remain a deadly threat to the city and the rule of law. Besides, he was eager to finish the job he had set himself and gratify to the limit his hatred of Gaius. So he sent one of the tribunes to kill Gaius' wife and daughter.

191 The tribune was Julius Lupus, a relative of Clemens. The reason they assigned the duty to him was that if he took part in the tyrannicide even to that extent, the citizen body would acclaim him for his valour and take him to be a colleague of those involved from the start in the whole plot.

192 Some of the conspirators thought it would be cruel, as well as rash, to vent their anger on the woman. Everything Gaius had done—all the disasters that had worn out the city and destroyed the flower of its citizens—he had done not on her advice but by

193 his own nature. But others accused her of deliberately bringing such things about, and attributed to her the whole responsibility for Gaius' evil acts. What sent him mad, they said, was a drug she gave him, calculated to enslave his mind and direct his passions to her; so it was she who had been the architect of total disaster

194 for the fortune of the Romans and their world empire. In the end, that view prevailed. Those who argued against it could do nothing to help her, and it was resolved that she should die.

So Lupus was sent, and lost no time in carrying out his commission. He did not want to be late in doing the bidding of those who sent him, or to incur blame in any way. After all, what he was doing was for the good of the people.

195 When he got to the residence, he found Gaius's wife Caesonia lying by her husband's body on the ground. Nothing had been done by way of customary tribute to the dead. She was stained with blood from his wounds and beside herself with misery. Her daughter was prostrate beside her.

Caesonia's only audible words in this extremity were to blame her husband for not believing her. 'I warned you, I warned you again and again!'

196   What she meant was disputed even at the time. (Similarly nowadays it depends on the hearers' attitude, since people attribute to it whatever significance they like.) Some said the words meant that she had warned him to give up his crazy behaviour and cruelty to the citizens, and to conduct his government with virtue and moderation, in case they should use his own methods, and kill him.

197   Others alleged that she had had word of the conspirators, and told Gaius not to delay but to secure his own safety by dealing with them all immediately, even if they had done nothing wrong; according to this version, her reproach meant that he had been too soft when she

198   warned him to take action. So much for what Caesonia said, and what people thought she meant.

Seeing Lupus approach, she pointed to Gaius' body and with

199   tears and lamentation beckoned him to come close. He did so, with a fixed purpose that showed his errand gave him pleasure. When she saw that, she knew why he had come. She bared her throat quite willingly and cried aloud, as people do cry in such manifest despair of life. 'Don't wait,' she told him—'finish the last act of the drama you have written for us.'

200   In this courageous manner she met her death. Lupus killed her daughter after her, and hurried off to report what he had done to Chaerea and the others.

VI

Obituary

201 Such was the end of Gaius. He had ruled Rome for four years less four months.

Even before he came to power he was perverse and ill-natured in the extreme—a slave to pleasure and a lover of malice, a man both paralysed in the face of fear and correspondingly murderous when in confident mood. Once he had his fill of power, he used it for one purpose only, the pursuit of outrageous violence.

Irrationally generous to those who least deserved it, he got his

202 wealth by murder and injustice. Determined to appear—and to be— superior to the laws of gods and men, he was a slave to the flattery of the people. Whatever the law calls wicked, and condemns, he regarded as the punishment of virtue.

203 He gave no thought to friendship, however close or well deserving, and would inflict punishment for even the most trivial things on those he was angry with. He reckoned to be at war with anything to do with virtue, and once he had conceived a desire there could be no opposition to whatever he ordered.

204 For instance, he used to sleep with his own sister—and it was that above all that caused the Romans' hatred of him to grow more violent. Such behaviour, unheard of for generations, provoked first disbelief and then loathing of the guilty man.

205 As for great imperial works undertaken for the benefit of contemporaries or posterity, not one can be attributed to Gaius. True, he had plans for a great harbour near Rhegium and Sicily to receive

206 the ships bringing corn from Egypt; that was certainly a splendid project, of the greatest benefit to navigation. But it never came to

207 anything. His plans lost their urgency and it was left half-finished, because his enthusiasm for useless expenditure on pleasures that

benefited no-one but himself took away his ambition for undeniably greater things.

208 For the rest, he was a first-rate orator, well trained in both Greek and Latin; replying off the cuff to other people's elaborate and long-prepared speeches, even on the weightiest subjects he could immediately show himself more persuasive than anyone. This was the result of a natural facility, strengthened by the application of 209 strenuous practice. Gaius had a strong motivation to devote himself to study: he was the great-nephew of Tiberius, his predecessor, who was famous for his accomplishments at a high scholarly level. Equally a lover of culture himself, and an apt pupil for his emperor-kinsman's instructions, Gaius was in the first rank among his contemporaries.

210 But the accumulated advantages of his education could not withstand the disastrous effect of power. So hard is it for those who can act casually and without responsibility to achieve the virtue of 211 self-control. At first, his studies and his ambition for honourable fame led him to choose thoroughly admirable people as his friends. But then excessive brutality robbed them of their goodwill towards him; hatred grew up instead, and it was their conspiracy against him that cost him his life.

VII

The Claudius Coup

212   I mentioned above that Claudius' route had diverged from that of Gaius. When the house was in uproar at the shock of a Caesar's death, Claudius squeezed into a narrow alley and hid there, not knowing what to do to save himself.

213

214   The only source of danger he suspected was his noble birth; for he was a private citizen of modest demeanour, satisfied with what he had, devoted to scholarship (especially in Greek), who distanced himself entirely from anything to do with trouble. But the crowd was now in the grip of panic, and the whole residence was full of soldiers on the rampage and civilians as cowardly and undisciplined as mercenary bodyguards.

   The cream of the Roman army are the soldiers called the Praetorians. They were holding a council of war about what should be done. Those present were not concerned about avenging Gaius—

215   he had deserved his fate—but were carefully considering how best their own interests might be served. (Even the Germans, who *were* engaged on vengeance against the assassins, did so not for the public good but to indulge their own savagery.)

216   Bewildered by all this, Claudius was afraid for his life—especially as he had seen the heads of Asprenas and the others being carried past. He stood back in the darkness in a place accessible by a few

217   steps. But he was seen by one of the palace guard.

   The soldier, whose name was Gratus, was able to make out that there was a person hiding, but because of the darkness could not recognise his face. He came closer. When Claudius tried to retreat, he caught hold of him, overpowered him, and then recognised who he was.

   'Here's a Germanicus!' he called to the soldiers behind; 'let's carry him off and set him up as emperor!'

218   Seeing they were all set to kidnap him, Claudius was terrified that he was going to die for the murder of Gaius. He begged them to spare him, pleading his inoffensive character; he had had no prior knowledge of what had been done.

219   Gratus grinned, and seized him by the hand. 'Stop snivelling about saving your life,' he said. 'Think big! The gods have taken power away from Gaius and given it to you, because you're a good man and they think of what's best for the world. So come on and take what's yours—the throne of your ancestors!'

220   In terror and joy at what he said, Claudius was completely incapable of walking. So Gratus picked him up and carried him.

221   By now more guardsmen were gathering. There were some black looks when they saw Claudius apparently being arrested and taken to execution for what had happened; after all, he had kept out of politics all his life and shared the dangers of Gaius' rule as much as anyone. Some of them thought the judgement on him should be referred to the consuls.

222   As more soldiers arrived the crowd panicked and fled, including even Claudius' litter-bearers, who despaired of their master's life when they saw him arrested and took the opportunity to save themselves. Claudius himself was in a state of physical collapse and could go no further.

223   By now they had reached the public area, and were in the open square on the Palatine—which is where, as the story goes, the city of Rome was first settled. There, a much larger assembly of soldiers greeted the sight of Claudius with joy, and insisted that he should be installed as emperor. For they had loved his brother Germanicus, whose glorious reputation lived on among all who had known him.

224   Calculation also entered into it. They knew how grasping the most powerful men in the Senate were, and how many things had
225 gone wrong the last time the Senate had been in power. A republic was unworkable, and if everything then changed back to the rule of one man, someone else's seizure of power could be dangerous for them. But Claudius could take it with their favour and support, and then, remembering his debt, pay them a reward appropriate to so great a gift.

226   These were the points they discussed with each other and reflected on individually. New contingents kept on arriving, who when the issues were explained to them enthusiastically endorsed the proclamation. So they closed ranks, wheeled round, picked up Claudius' litter for maximum speed, and carried him in it to the barracks.

227   A clear difference had emerged between the attitude of the senators and that of the people. The aim of the senators was to regain their former dignity; they owed it to their pride to free themselves, now that it was possible at last, from the slavery

228   imposed on them by the tyrants' insolence. The people, on the other hand, resented the Senate; they saw the emperors as a curb on its rapacity and a protection for themselves. They were delighted at the seizure of Claudius, believing that if he became emperor he would save them from the sort of civil strife there had been in the days of Pompey.

229   When the Senate heard that the soldiers had brought Claudius to the barracks, it sent to him a deputation consisting of those of its members whose moral integrity was most conspicuous. Their message was as follows. He must not hold power by violent means;

230   he should yield to the Senate, as one man outweighed by many, and let the rule of law look after the government of the state.

'Remember,' they went on, 'the damage done to Rome by previous tyrants. Remember the danger you were in yourself under Gaius, just as we were. You hated the burden of tyranny when others practised its insolence; don't now practise it yourself, by choosing to act like a drunken bully towards your country!

231   'If you listen to us, and show yourself determined to continue your blamelessly unpolitical life, you will receive honours by the votes of a free people. By giving the law its due, both ruler and ruled

232   earn praise for excellence. But if you lose your head, and learn no sense from the death of Gaius, we shall certainly not let you get away with it. A large part of the army is on our side, and we have stores of weapons and plenty of slaves to use them.

233   'Much depends on hope and chance. The gods only help those who strive on the side of goodness and honour—and that means those who fight for their country's freedom.'

234   Two of the envoys, Veranius and Brocchus, were also tribunes

of the *plebs*. When they had delivered their speech, they fell at Claudius' feet and begged him at all costs not to bring on the city the miseries of war. (They could see the size of the army that protected him; in comparison with that, the consuls were nothing.)

235 If he wanted power, let him accept it as a gift from the Senate: he would wield it with better fortune, and under better auspices, if it came to him not by violence but as a goodwill gift.

236 Claudius understood the arrogance of the Senate, and was momentarily swayed towards caution by what its envoys said. But two things enabled him to set aside his fear of it. The first was the confidence of the soldiers; the second was the advice of King Agrippa, not to let such power slip through his fingers when it came to him unbidden.

237 King Agrippa had been held in honour by Gaius, and did what was proper for him in return. He attended to the corpse, laid it on a bier, and did what he could to cover it. Then he withdrew to find the Praetorians. He told them that Gaius was alive but seriously wounded, and that doctors were on their way.

238 When he heard that Claudius had been seized by the soldiers, he pushed through the crowd to reach him. Claudius was in a state of confusion, ready to give way to the Senate, but Agrippa urged him on to claim the principate.

239 He had hardly returned home after giving this message when he was summoned to the Senate himself. Putting perfume in his hair, to make it appear that he was coming on after a party, he presented

240 himself before the senators and asked what Claudius had done. They told him what the situation was, and asked him in turn what he thought about it all.

He was ready, he said, to die for the honour of the Senate. But they should stop concentrating on what they would like, and look

241 instead to their own interests. For those who laid claim to power needed weapons and soldiers to protect them: it was dangerous to

242 do it unprepared. The reply was that the Senate would contribute money and an abundance of weapons. As for soldiers, it already had part of the army on its side, and would train more by giving slaves their freedom.

243   'Well, gentlemen,' said Agrippa, 'I hope you succeed. But I must speak frankly, for your security is at stake. I'm sure you know that the army that fights for Claudius has been trained in warfare for a great many years. Ours on the other hand will be a rabble: those who have just been unexpectedly released from slavery will not take kindly to discipline. We shall be fighting experts, when our

244   own troops hardly know how to draw their swords. So my advice is to send an embassy to Claudius in the hope of persuading him to lay down his power. I am willing to go myself as one of the envoys.'

245   This proposal was agreed, and Agrippa joined the embassy. But in private, he briefed Claudius about the Senate's disarray, and told him to give an imperious reply, as one who enjoyed the authority of power.

246   So Claudius replied as follows. He was not surprised, he said, that the Senate was unhappy at the imposition of a ruler, given the brutal treatment they had received at the hands of those who had previously held authority. But they would experience for themselves the moderation and justice of the days of *his* rule. The government would be monarchy in name, but in practice it would be open for all to share in common. They would do well to trust him in this, having seen with their own eyes the many vicissitudes he had been through.

247   With these conciliatory words the envoys were dismissed. Claudius then addressed the assembled troops, and made them swear on oath that they would be loyal to him. In return, he gave the Praetorian Guard five thousand denarii per man, with proportionately more for the officers, and promised similar sums to all the other armies.

248   While it was still night, the consuls summoned the Senate to meet in the temple of Jupiter the bringer of victory. The senators in hiding in the city were doubtful about obeying the summons. Those who had left for their country estates despaired of the liberty that had been won, because they foresaw how everything would turn out; they thought it better to live a life of ease free from the dangers of slavery than to risk their lives in winning the glory of

249 their ancestors. Even so, a hundred senators came to the meeting; but no more than that.

As they were discussing the situation, there was a sudden shout from the soldiers who were on their side: 'Choose a commander-
250 in-chief! Too many rulers will destroy the empire!' What mattered to them was that one man, and not everyone, should be in charge: they left it to the Senate to see who in particular was worthy of such great responsibility.

So the Senate's position had become even more painful; they were already afraid of Claudius, and now they had even lost the
251 liberty of which they were so proud. Even so, there were some among them whose illustrious birth and marriage connections made them ambitious. Marcus Vinicius, for example: distinguished for his own nobility, he was also the husband of Julia, the sister of Gaius. He was keen to make a bid for power, but the consuls restrained him by devising one pretext after another.
252 Valerius Asiaticus had similar ambitions, but he was checked by Minucianus, one of the assassins.

If these would-be emperors had been allowed to take up arms against Claudius there would have been a massacre without
253 parallel, not least because of the large number of gladiators in the city; these, with the soldiers of the night watch and the rowers from the fleet, were all streaming into the Praetorians' barracks. So the claimants withdrew, some to spare the city, others in fear for their own lives.

254 At daybreak, Chaerea and his companions came forward in the hope of addressing the soldiers. But when they raised their hands for silence and were about to speak, the crowd of soldiers shouted them down. They were all determined to be ruled by one man; they were calling for their new leader, and would not stand for any delay.
255 The Senate was paralysed. How to rule, when the soldiers would not respect them? How to be ruled, when Gaius' assassins would not let them give in to the soldiers?

256 Chaerea could not contain his fury. If they wanted an emperor, he'd give them one—let someone bring him the password from
257 Eutychus! (This Eutychus was a charioteer of the Green faction; Gaius, who was a fan of his, used to wear the soldiers out on the

humiliating forced labour of building stables for Eutychus' horses.)

258 With that, and many other such taunts, Chaerea challenged them to bring him the head of Claudius. How monstrous, to get rid of

259 a madman and then give power to an idiot! But his words had no effect. The soldiers drew their swords, raised their standards, and marched off to Claudius, to join in the oath of loyalty to him.

The Senate was left defenceless; the consuls had no more power

260 than private citizens. Aghast and dejected, not knowing how to behave in the face of Claudius' anger with them, the senators regretted what they had done and abused each other for it.

261 Then Sabinus, one of the assassins, stepped forward. He threatened to kill himself rather than set Claudius up as emperor and see a government of slaves take over. He accused Chaerea of cowardice, if after being the first to despise Gaius he now thought

262 his life worth living when it could not give Rome freedom. Chaerea replied that his resolve to die was not in doubt; however, he wanted to test Claudius' intentions thoroughly.

263 While the Senate was in a quandary, people were pressing towards the barracks from all sides, in order to pay their respects to Claudius.

Quintus Pomponius, one of the consuls, was especially guilty in the eyes of the soldiers, because he had summoned the Senate in the name of freedom. They drew their swords and rushed at him, and

264 would have killed him if Claudius had not prevented it. So Claudius rescued the consul, and found him a seat next to himself; but he had no such honourable welcome for the rest of the senators who had accompanied him. Some of them were punched by the soldiers, who shoved them away when they tried to approach Claudius. Aponius withdrew injured, and all of them were in danger.

265 King Agrippa went to Claudius and urged him to treat the senators more gently: if any harm should come to the Senate,

266 he would have no-one else to rule over. Claudius took the point, summoned the Senate to meet on the Palatine, and went there himself, carried through the city in his litter. The soldiers escorted him, with much brutality towards members of the public.

267 Of the killers of Gaius, Chaerea and Sabinus presented themselves openly, despite written orders confining them to their quarters

268 signed by Pollio, whom Claudius had just appointed commander of the guard. Claudius himself, on arrival at the Palatine, called his advisers and took a vote on Chaerea. Their view was that the deed had been a glorious one, but the man who did it was guilty of disloyalty; they thought it right that he should be punished as a deterrent for the future.

269 So Chaerea was taken out to execution, and with him Lupus and many other Romans. It is said that Chaerea bore his fate with dignity. His bearing was unmoved, and when Lupus turned and

270 wept, he rebuked him. Then, when Lupus stripped and complained of the cold, he told him that cold would never do a wolf any harm.

A crowd of spectators followed to the place of execution. Chaerea asked the soldier if he had had any practice at killing, or was this the first time he had held a sword? [...] 'Go,' he said, 'and fetch the sword I used to deal with Gaius.' Chaerea was fortunate, and died

271 at the first blow. Lupus, on the other hand, made a bad exit; he had not the courage to stretch his neck out firmly, and it took several strokes to kill him.

272 A few days later came the festival of offerings to the dead. The Roman people, having made sacrifice to their own dead relatives, burnt portions also in honour of Chaerea, appealing to his ghost to be gracious to them and not to be angry at their ingratitude.

273 So Chaerea ended his life. Sabinus, however, was exonerated by Claudius, and even allowed to keep his commission as an officer. But he thought it wrong that he had not kept faith with his comrades. So he killed himself, falling on his sword until the hilt touched the wound.

Note on the text

As the basis of the translation, I have used the text of Benedict Niese: *Flavii Iosephi opera* vol. 4 (Berlin 1890, repr. 1955) 211–58. In the following passages, however, identified by section and line number in Niese's text, I have preferred a different reading from his. For details of MSS, editions and emendations, see Niese's *apparatus criticus* and H. Schreckenberg, *Bibliographie zu Flavius Josephus* (Leiden 1968, supplement 1979).

	Niese's text	This translation	Source of reading
21.12	οὐ πάντ᾽ ἐλεύθερον	οὐκ ἀνελεύθερον	Hudson
22.14	ἐπ᾽ ἀλλήλων	ἐπ᾽ ἄλλων	Niese app. crit.
30.6	προσκαλεῖν	προσάπτειν	Schreckenberg
36.8	τοῦ	τοῦ τε	Niese app. crit.
37.10–11	τὸ ὅσον ἐπ᾽ αὐτοῖς γεγενημένοις	ὅσον ἐπ᾽ αὐτῷ γενόμενον	Hudson
43.13	ἀποδεδωκότος	ἐπιδεδωκότος	Thackeray
48.13	παραδιδόντος	παραδιδόντι	Bekker
52.6	ἀξιώσεων	δεξιώσεων	Schreckenberg
56.20	προσοίσομαι	προείσομαι	MS E (epitome)
68.18	εὐκτὸν	φευκτὸν	Bekker
69.20	χρήσασθαι	φυγῇ χρήσασθαι	Herwerden
72.10	τίμιον	σημεῖον	Hudson
74.18	αὐτοῖς	αὖθις	Holwerda
85.11	εἰώθει	ὠθεῖτο	Schreckenberg
90.5–6	ἀπειληφυίαις	ἀπειληφυίας	Naber
94.18	μανθάνει	μανθάνω	Shilleto
98.14	Ἀμβρώνας	Ἀσπρήνας	MS E (epitome)

	Niese's text	This translation	Source of reading
104.16	ἐπὶ τόπον	ἐπίτομον	Niese app. crit.
117.25–6	οἰκοδομηθησομένων	οἰκοδομησάμενων	ed. pr. (1544)
117.26	τῶν ἡμερῶν οἰκήσεις	τῶν μερῶν οἰκήσεως	ed. pr. (1544)
122.16	ἄθροισιν	ἀνδράσιν	Bekker
122.16	ἀρετήν	ἀρχήν	ed. pr. (1544)
123.20	Νωρβανὸς	Βάλβος Νωρβανὸς	Groag
137.3	ἀξιοῖεν	ἐξίοιεν	Hudson
144.6	τῆς χώρας	καὶ τῆς χαρᾶς	Hudson
148.19	παρῆν	περιῄει	Dindorf
150.4	συνεσόμενων	μὴ συνεσόμενων	Hudson
157.7	ὑπανίσως	ὑπανιεισῶν	Herwerden
157.11	πείσοιντο	ἀπέσοιντο	ed. pr. (1544)
178.16	τε	τε ἐστὲ	Hudson
180.21	νεώτερον	ἕτερον	Naber
182.4	δὲ	δὲ δεῖ	Dindorf
196.4	καὶ	μὴ	ed. pr. (1544)
196.4–5	παρ' αὐτὸν ... χρώμενον	παρ' αὐτῶν ... χρώμενων	Ernesti
203.8	τότε	τε	Niese app. crit.
212.2	κατειλημμένος	κατειλημένος	Schreckenberg
213.4	πᾶσιν	παροῦσιν	Terry
218.26	φωνὴν	φονήν	MS A (corr.)
221.10	ἀγόμενον	ἀγόμενον ἐσκυθρώπαζον	MS E (epitome)
221.13	ἐντρέπειν	ἐπιτρέπειν	MS E (epitome) and margin of A
225.5	δι' ἑνὸς	διά τινος	MSS W and M
225.6	παρ' ὃν	παρὸν	MSS A and W
234.19	Βρόγχος	Βρόκχος	Hudson
251.21	Μινουκιανὸς Μᾶρκον	Μᾶρκον Οὐινίκιον	Swan
263.15	θεραπείαν	θεραπείαν Κλαυδίου	MS A
272.24	αὐτῶν	αὐτῶν ἀπαρχὰς	Richards and Shutt

Commentary

1–16   J. links his account of Gaius' death to the overall theme of the *Antiquities,* and explains why he has treated it in such detail.

1   **The Jews in Jerusalem.**   J. refers back to *Ant.* XVIII 157–309 on Gaius' order to erect his statue in the temple at Jerusalem—a narrative in which King Agrippa plays a prominent part (XVIII 289–301). At XVIII 306–9, J. attributes Gaius' death to the providence of God in averting the sacrilege, and refers ahead (XVIII 307) to the present narrative, which will deal with 'the reason why he died and the nature of the plot against him'.

Outrageous madness.   Literally 'the madness of his *hybris*'. At *Bell.* II 184, J. applies the concept of *hybris* both to Gaius' acceptance of divine honours and to his sacrilegious plan for the Jerusalem statue. Madness was alleged by Philo (*Leg.* 34), Seneca (*Const.* 18.1), Dio (LIX 29.1), and by Claudius himself in his edict to Alexandria (quoted in *Ant.* XIX 284); it is also hinted at by Tacitus (*Ann.* XIII 3.2) and Suetonius (*Cal.* 50.2–3). J. takes it for granted in this introduction (1, 5, 11), but it is conspicuously absent from the obituary (201–11). Ferrill (158) insists that 'he was simply crazy', and his whole book is designed to refute modern attempts to argue the opposite. But Ferrill's own position largely depends on the tacit premise that cruelty, extravagance and irresponsibility necessarily connote madness.

Every land and sea.   Rhetorical hyperbole for Rome (2–4), the Bay of Naples (5–6) and Greece (7–10).

Rome's dominions.   'The administration of Gaius ... in the Empire at large does not appear, when scrutinized, to be lacking either in efficiency or sanity' (Balsdon 203). A less lenient view is taken by Ferrill 149–55.

2   **Persecuted the Senate.**   Details and discussion in Barrett 234–9, who somewhat unfairly blames the Senate itself for Gaius' autocratic arrogance.

Noble birth.   For instance, M. Iunius Silanus was forced to suicide, and Cn. Cornelius Lentulus Gaetulicus and M. Aemilius Lepidus put to death (Dio LIX 8.4–6, 22.5–6, Suet. *Cal.* 23.3, Seneca *Epistles* 4.7); other aristocrats were deliberately humiliated (Suet. *Cal.* 35.1, citing Cn. Pompeius Magnus, a Torquatus and a Cincinnatus).

3   **'Knights'.**   Nothing in the subsequent narrative justifies this emphasis on Gaius' treatment of the equestrian order in particular. See Barrett 232f on Gaius and the *equites* (unnecessarily trying to explain away the evidence for hostility).

Chosen from their number.   Cf. 24 (circus games), 75 (Augustus), 158 (Forum assemblies) and 202 (Praetorians) for similar explanations to non-Roman readers. On selection of senators, see Talbert 9–14.

Dishonour.   E.g. Dio LIX 10.1–2: twenty-six equestrians put to death by being compelled to fight as gladiators.

Plundered property.   E.g. Suet. *Cal.* 41.2: arbitrary arrests and confiscations. For Gaius' financial exactions see Dio LIX 14–15, Suet. *Cal.* 38–42.

4   **A god.**   Details in Dio LIX 26.5–28.8, Suet. *Cal.* 22.2–4, Philo *Leg.* 75–114; discussion in Balsdon 157–73, Ferrill 133–9, Barrett 140–53, none of whom, however, refers to Gaius' mystery-cult (see on 30 below).

Capitol.   Gaius is said to have begun building a house for himself in the *Area Capitolina* in front of the temple of Jupiter Optimus Maximus, and connected the Capitol to the Palatine with a 'bridge'—presumably a raised walkway—across the temple of Divus Augustus in the valley between (Suet. *Cal.* 22.4, Dio LIX 28.2).

Brother.   He called himself Jupiter Latiaris (Dio LIX 28.5, Suet. *Cal.* 22.2). Identification with Jupiter was appropriate in the light of his promiscuous adulteries and incestuous relations with his sisters (Dio LIX 26.5, Vict. *Caes.* 3.10).

5   **Dikaiarchia to Misenum.**   Dikaiarchia was the Greek name for Puteoli (modern Pozzuoli); Misenum, at the end of the promontory opposite, was the base of the Roman fleet (cf. J.'s reference to a warship). Suetonius (*Cal.* 19.1) and Dio (LIX 17.1) give a slightly shorter crossing, to Baiae or Bauli respectively. Details and discussion in Balsdon 51–4, Barrett 211–12, Ferrill 115–17.

Intolerable.   The Greek word *deinon* might mean 'dangerous'; and Gaius could not swim (Suet. *Cal.* 54.2).

6   **Lord of the sea**.   See Dio LIX 26.6 for Gaius as Neptune (cf. Suet. *Cal.* 52, dressing up with a trident). But the phrase could refer to his 'conquest of the Ocean' in the abortive British campaign: see Suet. *Cal.* 46 ('spoils of Ocean'), as explained by M.B. Flory, *Historia* 37 (1988) 498–504.

Three miles.   'Thirty *stadia*' (5.31 km), no doubt an approximate round number.

Appropriate to a god.   Hercules, later deified, had built the causeway across the Lucrine bay nearby: Strabo V 4.6 (245), Diodorus IV 22.2, Silius Italicus XII 114–19.

7   **Sculptures**.   For instance, Lysippus' bronze Eros from Thespiae (Pausanias IX 27.3), which was returned by Claudius but taken again by Nero and destroyed in the fire of 64.

8   **Decorated his house**.   For Greek masterpieces in the imperial palaces, see Millar 145.

Pheidias' statue.   According to Dio (LIX 28.3) and Suetonius (*Cal.* 22.2), he intended to replace the head with a portrait of himself and use it as the cult statue in his own temple.

9   **Memmius Regulus**.   I.e. P. Memmius Regulus, suffect consul in 31 and imperial legate of Moesia (with responsibility also for Macedonia and Achaea) from 35 to 44; in 38 he had been summoned to Rome to give his wife Lollia Paullina in marriage to Gaius (Suet. *Cal.* 25.2: Gaius soon divorced her, but Memmius did not get her back).

Portents.   The ship built to transport it was struck by lightning, and loud laughter frightened away the workmen dismantling the statue (Dio LIX 28.4, Suet. *Cal.* 57.1). For the manipulation of such miracles, see G.W. Bowersock in *Opposition et résistances à l'Empire d'Auguste à Trajan* (Fondation Hardt vol. 33, Geneva 1987) 294–304.

10 **Only survived**.   Like P. Petronius in Syria (*Ant.* XVIII 304–9) and Apollonius the Egyptian at Rome (Dio LIX 29.4).

11 **Daughter**.   Julia Drusilla, born one month after Gaius' marriage to Milonia Caesonia (Dio LIX 23.7, 28.7, Suet. *Cal.* 25.3–4), probably in the early summer of 39 (Barrett 94–6).

Capitol.   Dio (LIX 28.7) and Suetonius (*Cal.* 25.4) add that Gaius appointed Minerva, who shared the Capitoline temple with Jupiter and Juno, as the baby's nurse.

12   **Incited the slaves.** See 131 below. J. makes this the origin of the
          conspiracies (14), a motivation not borne out in his main narrative.

13   **Polydeuces.** Suetonius (*Claud.* 9.1) refers to Claudius being hounded
          by prosecutions, 'even by one of his own servants'. Cf. 67, Gaius' alleged
          urging of Claudius' freedman Callistus to poison him. Jung (374–5)
          takes this as evidence of Claudius' political importance; more likely, I
          think, of Gaius' malice (cf. Seneca *Apocolocyntosis* 15.2).
          Not how it turned out. At 68 (on Callistus), J. reasonably points out
          that if Gaius had really wanted Claudius dead, he would have made
          sure it happened.

14   **Slaves to rule.** J.'s word is *doulokratia,* as also at 261 (Sabinus) and
          in a Byzantine encyclopaedia (*Suda* s.v. 'Gaios'). Dio (LX 2.4) uses the
          verb form to describe Claudius' dependence on his freedmen.
          Many plots. According to Suetonius (*Cal.* 56.1), 'one or two were
          discovered, and the others were held up for lack of opportunity'
          when Chaerea and Sabinus (see on 46 below) formed their successful
          conspiracy. Barrett (155–62) is too keen to make them all part of a
          single process.
          Before they fell. E.g. Vinicianus (20, 49f).

15   **For the laws.** The laws represent constitutional government, the
          opposite of tyranny (156, 172f; cf. 57, 74, 230f; Lucan VII 440); together
          with 'liberty', they define the Republic (Wiseman *KC* 2–3, Wirszubski
          7–9, 83–7). Compare Cicero *De lege agraria* 2.102 (in a speech to the
          People): 'your liberty is based on the laws'.
          Our own nation. See on 1 above for the context.
          An exact account. The phraseology is reminiscent of Thucydides
          (I 22.2, V 26.5).

16   **Power of God.** See *Ant.* XVIII 127 (on Herod), 284 and 305f (on
          Petronius and the statue); also 61 and 69 below (contrast 72, where the
          reference to the gods must come from J.'s source).
          A lesson in prudence. For historiography as a source of moral
          instruction, see for instance Polybius II 61.3, Diodorus I 1, Cicero
          De oratore II 36 (*magistra vitae*), Livy pref. 10. It is characteristic of J.
          to be explicit about it (cf. XVII 60, etc).

17–23   J. begins his 'exact account' with an analysis of the conspiracies
          mentioned at 14. But it is inconsistent with his main narrative, centred

on Chaerea: note (*a*) the repeated explanations of the motivation of Vinicianus (20/49) and Chaerea (21/29–31), (*b*) the prominence of Aemilius Regulus, who is not mentioned again, and (*c*) the clear implication that the three sets of conspirators were collaborating, which as far as Chaerea and Vinicianus are concerned contradicts the narrative at 49–59.

17   **Aemilius Regulus.**   Otherwise unknown; it is probably a coincidence that the patrician Aemilii used the similar *cognomen* 'Regillus'. See Bernard J. Kavanagh, *Historia* 50 (2001) 379–84, for the suggestion that the name should be 'Aemilius Rectus', and the conspirator a relative of Seneca.

Cordoba.   Principal city of Hispania Ulterior; for the cultural background, see Miriam Griffin, *Journal of Roman Studies* 62 (1972) 1–19. Seneca came from Cordoba, and Ritter (89 n. 34) points out that the historian Fabius Rusticus was a friend of Seneca and probably from Spain himself (Tac. *Ann.* XIII 20.2, cf. Syme *Tac.* 179–80); if this passage is from Fabius Rusticus, then the main narrative is due to someone else.

18   **Cassius Chaerea.**   The hero of the main narrative, which begins with his motivation (27–37), ends with his death (267–73), and insists on his primacy (111–13); here he is merely one of three, with an essentially auxiliary role.

Military tribune.   Mentioned by Tacitus as a fiery young centurion at the time of the Rhine army mutinies in 14, Chaerea must have been in his early fifties in 41. He was now *tribunus cohortis praetoriae* (Suet. *Cal.* 56.2), i.e. commander of one of the nine cohorts of the Praetorian Guard. See Millar 61f, and Lawrence Keppie, *The Making of the Roman Army* (London 1984) 187; on equestrian officers in general, Eric Birley, *Roman Britain and the Roman Army* (Kendal 1953) 133–53.

Annius Minucianus.   I.e. L. Annius Vinicianus, the proper form of whose name is known from the Acts of the Arval Brethren (Smallwood nos. 4 and 10) and from Tac. *Ann.* VI 9.3 and Dio LX 15.1. J. names him twelve times and calls him 'Minucianus' every time; since it is clearly his own error rather than manuscript corruption, I have let it stand in the text. Son of C. Annius Pollio (Tac. *Ann.* VI 9.3), who was probably consul in 21 or 22, Vinicianus was no doubt in his thirties or early forties in 41. He had evidently been consul himself (to judge by

J.'s description of him at 52), but the date is not known. His *cognomen* implies a close family link with M. Vinicius, Gaius' brother-in-law (Barrett 33, 108); certainly he was on familiar terms with the emperor (cf. 96–7).

19 **Not … kept secret.**   Cf. 62, 91f, 132f; on the other hand, secrecy is stressed at 48, 51 and 112.

Many of his friends.   Including Fabius Rusticus? See on 17 above.

20 **Lepidus.**   I.e. M. Aemilius Lepidus, son of the M. Lepidus (consul in AD 6) whom Augustus is said to have judged capable of the principate (Tac. *Ann.* I 13.2); nephew of the L. Aemilius Paullus (consul in AD 1) who married Augustus' grand-daughter Julia and was exiled for conspiracy in AD 8 (Suet. *Augustus* 19.1); and brother of the Aemilia Lepida who had been married to Gaius' brother Drusus (Tac. *Ann.* VI 40.3). Himself the husband of Gaius' sister Drusilla, Lepidus enjoyed the favours of Livilla and Agrippina too, and was allegedly Gaius' own homosexual partner (Dio LIX 11.1, 22.6, Suet. *Cal.* 36.1). Gaius said he would make Lepidus his heir, and allowed him to hold office five years below the legal age, but in 38 he executed him for treason, alleging complicity, as well as adultery, on the part of Livilla and Agrippina (Dio LIX 22.7–9, Suet. *Cal.* 24.3, Tac. *Ann.* XIV 2.2).

Lepidus' execution is associated with that of Cn. Lentulus Gaetulicus, consul in 26 and imperial legate of Upper Germany since 29, the detection of whose 'criminal plots' against Gaius was celebrated with sacrifice by the Arval Brethren on 27 October 39 (Smallwood no. 9, Suet. *Claud.* 9.1, Dio LIX 22.5f. See Barrett 81–3, 101–13; Syme *AA* 179f, with chapters 8–10 and stemmata 4 and 5 on the Aemilii Lepidi in general. See also on 18 above: Vinicianus' presumed relative M. Vinicius, consul in 30, was the husband of Livilla (Tac. *Ann.* VI 15.1).

21 **Effeminacy.**   See below, 29–31; Suet. *Cal.* 56.2, Dio LIX 29.2, Sen. *Const.* 18.3 (who says Chaerea really did seem effeminate), Pausanias IX 27.3 (who takes Gaius' death at Chaerea's hands as the vengeance of Eros).

On close terms.   As a Praetorian officer.

22 **By common consent.**   Contrast the psychologically more convincing account in the main narrative (below, 51 and 112). But both the text and the meaning of this sentence are very uncertain; the sixth-century Latin translator, who clearly had a very different version in front of him, renders it 'The rest were eager in addition to have a common plan, seeing such injustices and the evil example that was being given to those who wanted the position of emperor'.

23   **Easier for an officer.** Timpe (*UK* 79–81, cf. *RG* 494) believes that Chaerea was merely the agent for a conspiracy of senators who 'pulled the strings' in the background. All the evidence, including both the versions J. uses, suggests otherwise.

24–31   J. evidently changes his source at this point. The main narrative, centred on Chaerea, identifies the moment when he decided to act.

24   **Chariot races.** Probably the *ludi Romani,* which were held from 4 to 19 September; the last five days were devoted to chariot-racing. See H.H. Scullard, *Festivals and Ceremonies of the Roman Republic* (London 1981) 183–8.

    Petition emperors. See for instance Tac. *Ann.* VI 13, Suet. *Augustus* 34.2, *Tiberius* 47, Pliny *NH* XXXIV 62, Dio LIX 13.3–7; and in general Alan Cameron, *Circus Factions* (Oxford 1976) ch. 7.

25   **Taxes.** Increased by Gaius to pay for his extravagances (Suet. *Cal.* 40–1, Dio LIX 28.8–11); on Gaius' finances, see Balsdon 180–9, Barrett 224–9.

26   **Many people were killed.** So too Dio LIX 28.11.

27   **More determined.** J.'s attempt to reconcile his sources? At 18–23 Chaerea's plan is already made; the main narrative, on the other hand, implies that he decided to act at 27 and to seek allies at 32.

28   **Rate had been doubled.** Not otherwise attested. (Nor is Chaerea's responsibility for enforcing payment.)

29   **Some humiliating word.** See on 21 above: Seneca and Suetonius offer 'Priapus' and 'Venus'; Dio's version is 'Desire' (*pothos*) and 'Aphrodite'; Pausanias perhaps implies 'Eros'. Robert Graves (*I Claudius*, Penguin ed. 385) suggests some more picturesque phrases.

30   **He himself.** Seneca (*Const.* 18.3), making the same point, describes Gaius as wearing transparent clothes, Greek sandals and gold ornaments.

    Mystery-cult. See 71 and 104 below. A tenth-century encyclopaedia (*Suda*, s.v. 'Gaios') refers to Gaius wearing women's clothes and false hair, acting as a woman and 'carrying out every sort of obscenity', in the context of his invention of initiation rites and celebration of 'foreign mysteries'. The item probably derives ultimately from Dio, whose surviving abbreviated text (LIX 26.5–10) associates Gaius' impersonation of gods and goddesses with the 'supplications, prayers and sacrifices' that were offered to him. Gaius introduced to Rome the forms of emperor worship customary in the Greek East, one of which was mystery-cult; see H.W. Pleket, *Harvard Theological Review* 58 (1965) 331–47, for the features of this form of worship, including hymns, dance, sacred drama, impersonation of divine characters, and a nocturnal ritual that probably culminated in the revelation and adoration of the image of the emperor-god.

Gaius' dance performance at dead of night before three senior senators (Suet. *Cal.* 54.2, Dio LIX 5.5) is probably to be understood in this context, as is his transvestism (Suet. *Cal.* 52, Dio LIX 26.6f, Vict. *Caes.* 3.12) and divine impersonations. His dressing up as a Maenad with wine-cup and thyrsus (Dio LIX 26.7) may suggest that the mysteries were Dionysiac in nature; but if he was Liber—i.e. Dionysus—for his Bacchanalian dancing, he was also Jupiter for his sexual habits (Vict. *Caes.* 3.10); and he was all the other gods and goddesses as well (Philo *Leg.* 75–114, Dio LIX 26.6). When Gaius' sister-consort Drusilla died in June 38, he deified her as *Panthea* (Dio LIX 11.3), and he seems to have developed his own cult with the same idea in mind. For gods with many names, see Ramsay MacMullen, *Paganism in the Roman Empire* (Yale 1981) 86–91.

31   **His turn.**   I.e. when his cohort was on duty at the Palatine?

32–48   The Quintilia episode drives Chaerea to seek allies.

32   **Pompedius.** 'Pompidius' in the sixth-century Latin translation, 'Pomponius' at Dio LIX 26.4, anonymous at Suet. *Cal.* 16.4; sometimes identified with the Pompeius Pennus mentioned by Seneca (*De beneficiis* II 12). 'Poppaedius' is a possible correction: cf. Diodorus XXXVII 2.9 for the corruption of that name into 'Pompaedius'. P.M. Swan, *Phoenix* 30 (1976) 54–60, accepts Dio's version of the name and identifies the senator as Publius Pomponius Secundus, brother of the consul referred to at 263 below and himself consul in AD 44; Tacitus' comment about the elegance of his life (*Ann.* v 8.2) could be a reference to Epicureanism. Galimberti on the other hand (175–6) rules Pomponius out on the unsupported belief that he was a Stoic.

Epicurean. For the Epicureans' doctrine on social life, including non-involvement in politics, see A.A. Long and D.N. Sedley, *The Hellenistic Philosophers* (Cambridge 1987) 1.1125–39.

33   **Timidius**. Unknown. The name is unparalleled, probably (as usual in J.) the result of textual corruption. 'Timinius' is the closest attested Roman name. Possibly 'Ummidius', i.e. Gaius Ummidius Durmius Quadratus, consul c. 40 (Birley 620–2).

Quintilia. A freedwoman (Suet. *Cal.* 16.4), as were most of her profession. Compare the popular Quinctia of *Priapea* 27: W.H. Parker, *Priapea: Poems for a Phallic God* (London 1988) 113.

34   **Torture**. Theoretically illegal when inflicted on a Roman citizen; but emperors could do what they liked, and Gaius was particularly sadistic (Seneca *De ira* III 18.3–19.5, Suet. *Cal.* 27–8, 30.1).

35   **One of those involved**. In what? The phrase presupposes an actual plot (so too Suet. *Cal.* 16.4), which Timpe (*UK* 79 n. 2) and Barrett (158) assume was Chaerea's own conspiracy. But that is inconsistent with J.'s narrative at this point.

Gaius' presence. The hearing, and the torture, presumably took place in the emperor's private quarters: see Seneca *Natural Questions* IVa 17.

36   **Acquitted**. If 'Pompedius' was Pompeius Pennus (see on 32 above), he prostrated himself in gratitude and kissed Gaius' golden sandal.

Gift of money. 800,000 sesterces, according to Suetonius (*Cal.* 16.4).

37   **Done his best**. Text and meaning very uncertain.

Clemens. I.e. M. Arrecinus Clemens (Tac. *Hist.* IV 68.2, Suet. *Titus* 4.2): see on 154 below. There were two Praetorian Prefects, both suspect to Gaius according to Dio (LIX 25.7–8); the name of Clemens' colleague is not known, but Arruntius Stella is a possibility (see on 148 below). Jung (384f) and Levick (37f) offer rival—and equally speculative—theories about their respective motives.

Papinius. Otherwise unknown. Conceivably related to the Sex. Papinius who was put to death by Gaius (Seneca *De ira* III 18.3), a son of Sex. Papinius Allenius, consul in 36.

40   **Without fear**. As the sequel shows (47, 191), Chaerea and his fellow-conspirators did not know whether they could trust Clemens. But he was said later to have been involved in the plot (Suet. *Cal.* 56.1, Dio LIX 29.1), and Claudius replaced him (267); see on 154 below.

42	**Bodyguards.** I.e. no better than the Germans (119–21). But that had been the essential role of the Praetorian Guard from the beginning (Dio LIII 11.5); see Millar 61f.
	Freedom and sovereignty. The first indication of Chaerea's republicanism: see below, 46, 57, 74 etc (Wiseman *KC* 2–5).
43	**He suspects us.** As a result of the false confession of Betilienus Capito: Dio LIX 29.7–8, cf. Suet. *Cal.* 56.1.
	His own pleasure. Seneca (*De ira* III 18.3) and Suetonius (*Cal.* 32.1) give examples of his sadistic entertainments; but there is a more general point here, that tyrants are motivated by personal whim rather than public responsibility (172 below).
44	**His approval.** See on 40 above.
	Keep quiet. See on 19 above; another inconsistency between J.'s sources.
46	**Cornelius Sabinus.** Dio (LIX 29.1) and Suetonius (*Cal.* 58.2) give him equal status with Chaerea in the formation of the plot. Contrast 111–13: J.'s main source concentrates on Chaerea alone (Timpe *RG* 494).
48	**Kept silent.** Text and meaning uncertain. The Greek seems to say 'entrusted their affairs to silence'; the Latin translator, more logically, has 'did not reveal his own opinion on such a matter'.

49–63	Chaerea and Sabinus enlist Vinicianus as the leader of their cause. Timpe (see on 23 above) believes that Vinicianus was 'pulling the strings' from the start; Barrett (162), influenced by this hypothesis, describes J.'s narrative here as 'most implausible'. But that is to prefer preconception to evidence. Why should we suppose that J.'s source was mistaken, and that Chaerea was a mere puppet?
49	**Minucianus.** I.e. Vinicianus: see on 18 above.
	Excellence of character. A Thucydidean phrase (VII 86.5, on Nicias).
	Lepidus. See on 20 above.
50	**Rage.** Literally 'madness' (*mania*): see on 1 above.
51	**Fear of danger.** Gaius' hostility to the Senate was particularly acute at the time of his return from Germany in 40 (Suet. *Cal.* 49.1).
52	**High nobility.** Vinicianus must have been descended from the consular Annii of the Republic (T. Annius Luscus, T. Annius Rufus, consuls in 153 and 128 BC); the Vinicii were of more recent nobility (Tac. *Ann.* VI 15).

53   **Password.**   See on 29 above.

54   **Liberty.**   Brutus' password at Philippi (Dio XLVII 43.1).

55   **Before this meeting.**   How far had Vinicianus got in sounding out sympathisers? Not very far, to judge by 51.

57   **Of no significance.**   Borne out at 100 and 269 below.

60   **Entering the Senate-house.**   It was one of the Praetorians' duties to guard the Senate (Dio LVIII 9.5).

       A voice was heard.   For mysterious voices bearing supernatural messages, see Cicero *De divinatione* I 109, with A.S. Pease's commentary (Urbana 1920, p. 279). As a priest, J. himself was skilled in interpreting divine utterances (*Bell.* III 352 etc).

61   **The first encouragement.**   Text and meaning uncertain: some MSS omit 'first' (*proton*).

       God.   See on 16 above.

62   **Reached many people.**   As a result of the involvement of Vinicianus? This stage of events is no doubt the equivalent of 22 above (from a different source).

63   **Eager not to fall short.**   Compare 22 above.

       To kill a tyrant.   The first appearance of the word in J.'s narrative; it occurs sixteen times (most conspicuously at 92, 155, 176–7 and 187) in the part of the text attributable to J.'s main source, but otherwise only twice (227 and 230), where the Senate's view is reported. Tyrannicide was a concept borrowed from Greek philosophy by the *optimates* in the late Republic, in order to justify political assassination (Wiseman *KC* 5–8).

64–9   Callistus' knowledge of the plot. See Dio LIX 29.1, Tac. *Ann.* XI 29.1; cf. Suet. *Cal.* 56.1 ('the most powerful freedmen'). Levick (36–9), following Jung (373–5), uses this passage as evidence for an otherwise unattested plan to replace Gaius with Claudius. But Callistus' claim to have backed Claudius (66f) cannot bear so much weight. As J. himself saw (68f), that was merely what he said afterwards, to claim credit. If there *was* a plot to make Claudius emperor, then the plotters signally failed to produce their man when it mattered (212–20 below). It seems to me an implausible hypothesis.

       Birley (620 n. 1) notes that 'the anti-Claudian freedmen motif is very pronounced here; and the whole section looks rather like an insertion'.

The Death of Caligula

He therefore suggests that it should be attributed to Fabius Rusticus. Galiberti, on the other hand (179), suggests that 66–9 might come from Claudius' autobiography (Suet. *Claud.* 41.3).

64   **Callistus.**   I.e. C. Iulius Callistus (Millar 75): the full name is given by the medical writer Scribonius Largus, who dedicated his *Compositiones* to him (pref. 1, 12–14).

        Vast wealth.   He built himself a house with thirty onyx columns in the dining room (Pliny *NH* XXXVI 60).

65   **Arrogance.**   Seneca (*Epistles* 47.9) had seen Callistus' former master queuing vainly for admission at his door.

        Abuse of power. See Dio LIX 19.6 for his influence with Gaius, and Millar 69–83 on imperial freedmen in general.

        Could never be swayed.   See Suet. *Cal.* 29.1 on Gaius' *adiatrepsia*.

66   **Paid court to Claudius.**   Cf. Levick 34: 'Fear for his wealth is the reason given; a better explanation is that he saw Gaius as a danger to himself and likely to fall victim to a conspiracy, and prepared for the future. For him that must be by preparing for a new master in the family: Claudius.' But how credible an emperor was Claudius before 41? Levick and Jung do their best to make him a realistic candidate, but the judgement of Augustus and Tiberius suggests otherwise (Suet. *Claud.* 4–5).

        Prestige and power.   Callistus was later notorious as one of the three principal freedmen-counsellors of Claudius: see Tac. *Ann.* XI 29.2, 38.4, XII 1–2, and Pliny *NH* XXXIII 134.

67   **Deal with Claudius.**   See on 13 above.

        I think.   From the source, or J.'s own contribution? See 107 for a similar expression.

69   **Heavenly power.**   See on 16 above. Gratus too attributed it to the gods (219).

70–83   Delays and postponements, from September 40 (24 above) to January 41. The effect of the narrative is to heighten the suspense and bring out the contrast between Chaerea's boldness and the caution, or cowardice (112 below), of the rest. Timpe (*UK* 79) infers that since Chaerea was not in control of the timing of the attempt, his role was a subordinate one; but that is unlikely in itself (see on 23 above) and inconsistent with Dio LIX 29.5–6.

71   **Daughter.**   See on 11 above. The particular occasions for sacrifice are not known.

          Basilica.   I.e. the Basilica Julia on the south-west side of the Forum (Suet. *Cal.* 37.1); if J. had meant 'the palace' (thus Feldman 249 and Barrett 292 n. 7), he would have said *basileion,* not *basilike.*

          Throwing gold and silver coins.   See Millar 135–9 on imperial munificence.

          Mystery-cult.   See on 30 above. It is not known where the rites took place.

72   **Oblivious to everything.**   A Thucydidean phrase (I 41.2, speech of Corinthians at Athens).

          Sign from heaven.   Literally 'from the gods' (see on 16 above), but the text is uncertain.

73   **Chaerea was furious.**   Compare Cethegus' impatience with his fellow-conspirators in Sallust *Catiline* 43.3.

74   **More on his guard.**   As happened after the discovery of an earlier conspiracy (Dio LIX 25.6–8).

75   **Palatine Games.**   The *ludi Palatini* (Suet. *Cal.* 56.2) were instituted by Livia in 14 in honour of the deified Augustus (Dio LVI 46.5, cf. Tac. *Ann.* I 73). It was a 'private festival', as opposed to the publicly-funded *Augustalia* on 3–12 October, and was held annually on the Palatine for three days beginning on 17 January. That was Augustus' and Livia's wedding anniversary, and also the date of the annual sacrifices at the altar to the *Numen* of Augustus which Tiberius had dedicated, probably in AD 9: the evidence of the calendars is summarised in Ehrenberg and Jones, *Documents Illustrating the Reigns of Augustus and Tiberius* (ed. 3, Oxford 1976) 46. It is reasonable to infer that the festival was held at or near the altar (87 and 142 below).

          First transferred power.   I.e. Augustus. J.'s explanation (see on 3 above) is inconsistent with the view his source attributes to the consul and senators at 173 and 187 (Julius Caesar, 59 BC).

          From the Republic.   Literally 'from the people [*demos*]'; authors writing in Greek frequently use *demokratia* to refer to the Republic (see on 162 below), although it was far from a democracy. In fact, the Caesars claimed to have freed the people from the domination of an aristocratic oligarchy (Caesar *De bello civili* I 22.5, Augustus *Res gestae* 1.1); and that is the position implied at 228 below.

A wooden hut. Evidently used as part of the temporary theatre (see 90 below). There were two historic wooden huts on the Palatine: one was the so-called 'house of Romulus' at the top of the steps leading down from the temple of Victory to the Circus Maximus (Dionysius I 79.11, Plutarch *Romulus* 20.5), sometimes attributed to Cacius or Faustulus (Diodorus IV 21.2, Solinus 1.18) and evidently used as a club-house for the Priests of the Great Mother (Philodemus in *Anthologia Palatina* VII 222.3); the other was the so-called *auguratorium*, the hut on the summit of the hill from which Romulus took the inaugural auspices for his new foundation (Dionysius II 5.1–2). The latter, also known as the hut of Mars (Dionysius XIV 2.2, Plutarch *Camillus* 32.4), the *curia* of the Salii (Cicero *De divinatione* I 30) or the hut of Faustulus (Zonaras VII 3, Tzetzes on Lycophron *Alexandra* 1232), is much the more likely to be the one mentioned here.

In front of the imperial residence. See Appendix 1 for the pre-Neronian Palatine. I have translated J.'s *basileion* as 'imperial residence', in order not to give the false impression of a purpose-built palace. It consisted of a group of separate houses (see on 104 and 117 below), with a formal entrance and a wide forecourt, evidently opening on to a piazza (223 below). It was normal practice for a temporary stage and seats to be set up at the appropriate site for the duration of a festival (Dio XXXVII 58.4, Servius on Virgil *Georgics* 3.34).

The emperor. Literally 'Caesar'—the name used as a title, as at 97, 122 and 212 below.

Roman nobility. Not they alone: see 86 below.

76 **His guards.** J.'s term *hypaspistai*, used of the elite corps of Alexander the Great's army, suggests that he means here not the Germans (119–21) but the Praetorian Guard itself. The doubt about their loyalty to Gaius is appropriate, since at least three of the plotters were Guards officers.

77 **Fortuitous delays.** According to Timpe (*RG* 494), J.'s reference to chance disguises the deliberate caution of Chaerea's senatorial masters. But 78 and 80 clearly reveal Chaerea as the leader.

Three days were added. The MSS reading, 'exceeding the three by the scheduled days', is unintelligible. No satisfactory emendation has been offered, but the reference must be to Gaius' three-day extension of the festival (Dio LIX 29.6). This was to enable Gaius himself 'to dance and to act a tragedy', evidently as part of his mystery-cult (see on 30 above);

according to Suetonius (*Cal.* 54.2, 57.4), he had ordered an all-night festival as the occasion of his first public performance, and a drama with scenes in the underworld was being rehearsed. Both items are appropriate to mystery cults.

79   **Happiness.**   See 15 above.

Honour and admiration.   Fame is the spur, as it was for Hector (*Iliad* XXII 304f) and even for Cicero (*Pro Archia* 26, 28f).

81   **Alexandria.**   For the planned visit (surely not in January?), see Suet. *Cal.* 49.2, Philo *Leg.* 172f, 250–3, 338: he expected a more appreciative public there for his divinity. An alternative tradition (Suet. *Cal.* 51.3) evidently claimed that he was planning to flee as a result of news of a revolt in Germany; that was probably influenced by Nero's plan to go to Alexandria in 68 (Suet. *Nero* 47.2, Dio LXII 18.1, LXIII 27.2).

Disgracing.   Cf. Tac. *Hist.* I 82.1, 'contra decus imperii' (on Otho).

82   **Some Egyptian.**   'Egyptians generally were regarded by the Romans with hatred and contempt' (J.P.V.D. Balsdon, *Romans and Aliens* [London 1979] 68); in particular, they were thought of as cowardly and treacherous (Florus IV 2.60 etc). But we know from a contemporary source (Philo's essay *That Every Good Man is Free* 141) that theatre audiences in Alexandria would rise and cheer at lines praising liberty.

83   **A man with any pride.**   Thus Pericles in the Funeral Speech (Thucydides II 43.6).

84–98   The last chance.

85   **At dawn.**   Presumably 22 January, the last day of the extended festival. Suetonius (*Cal.* 58.1), whose MSS vary between 24, 25 and 26 January, must be mistaken.

Proper equipment.   The cavalryman's sword was for slashing, not stabbing; and Chaerea uses it when he asks for the password (105 below).

Chaerea's turn.   But see on 105 below.

86   **Not set aside.**   For the normal distinctions of seating, see Suet. *Augustus* 44, with Elizabeth Rawson, *Papers of the British School at Rome* 55 (1987) 83–114. But the *ludi Palatini* were the private benefaction of the imperial house (75 above); and in any case Gaius would do what he wanted. Timpe (*UK* 78) sees it as an example of his deliberate humiliation of the elite (cf. Suet. *Cal.* 26.2).

Women. See Rawson, pp. 89–91. They were usually segregated at the back.

Slaves. See Rawson, pp. 87–9. They usually had to stand.

87 **Sacrificed.** At the altar to the *Numen* of Augustus (see on 75 above)? **Sacrificial animals.** Suetonius (*Cal.* 57.4) specifies that Gaius sacrificed a flamingo, and was spattered with blood himself. Flamingoes were among the exotic victims sacrificed in Gaius' own cult (Suet. *Cal.* 22.3). **Asprenas.** I.e. P. Nonius Asprenas, consul in 38. He may have been involved in the plot: see on 98 below.

Butchered. See 123 below.

88 **Uncharacteristic.** For his usual grimness and bad temper, see Suet. *Cal.* 25.4, 50.1, Tac. *Ann.* xv 72.2.

89 **Friends.** E.g. Vinicianus (96), Asprenas? (98), Claudius, M. Vinicius, D. Valerius Asiaticus, Paullus Arruntius (102).

90 **Put up every year.** See on 75 above.

Portico. I.e. the Ionic colonnade on the 'Sorrento base'? See Appendix 1.

Go in and out. I.e. into and out of the imperial complex (*basileion*, 75)?

The hut itself. See on 75 above.

Another room. Text and meaning very uncertain. Naber's emendation (p. 41 above) is supported by the Latin version: 'there is also another chamber (*cella*) there, where actors and singers usually practise.'

Partitions. The phraseology echoes Thucydides (i 133, on Pausanias at Sparta); so even if we could be sure what J. wrote, there would still remain the question how well he understood his source, and whether he was influenced in his interpretation of it by the Thucydidean reminiscence.

91 **Extremity.** Literally 'horn'; cf. Pliny *NH* xxxiv 26 for the 'horns' (*cornua*) of the Comitium, which was roughly theatre-shaped. The 'extremities' of the semicircular auditorium must have been closest to the side exits, the right-hand one presumably leading into the imperial complex (see on 90). Gaius' convenience, and perhaps security, dictated his choice of seat, which must have obliged the performers to play to their left rather than straight out to the main audience.

Bathybius. The name is unparalleled, un-Roman, and clearly corrupt, but no likely emendation has yet been offered. Ritter (86f) suggests 'Talthybius', the name of Agamemnon's herald in the *Iliad* and therefore appropriate for one who, as it were, announces the programme; that would imply a learned joke in the source (cf. Seneca *Apocolocyntosis* 13.1 on Mercury as 'the Talthybius of the gods'), which J. has misunderstood. Ingenious but far-fetched—and even if it were right, the real name of the ex-praetor remains unknown. Birley (622–3) suggests 'Pacuvius', the acting governor of Syria under Tiberius (Seneca *Letters* 12.8, Tac. *Ann.* II 79.2).

Cluvius. I.e. presumably the historian Cluvius Rufus (see Appendix 2), who was certainly an ex-consul in 65 (Suet. *Nero* 21.2). The fact that he was imperial legate in Spain in 69 (Tac. *Hist.* I 8) does not necessarily rule out a pre-41 date for his consulship.

Ever since Mommsen 120 years ago, 'it has been argued (and most believe without question) that Cluvius the consular is none other than Cluvius Rufus the historian: an anecdote of this kind can derive only from Cluvius Rufus himself, and not verbally, but precisely from his writings. None the less, some cause for hesitation will subsist ...' (Syme *Tac.* 287, cf. 293f). Mommsen's article was in *Hermes* 4 (1870) 295–325, reprinted in *Gesammelte Schriften* 7 (1909) 224–52. Timpe (*RG* 500f) objects that a personal reference on so insignificant a detail is more appropriate to memoirs than to history proper. But we cannot be dogmatic about the observance of such conventions: certainly Velleius Paterculus (II 104.3f) did not feel inhibited about using his own eye-witness testimony in his history. The vividness, precision and psychological authenticity of the scenes in the theatre (86–98, 127–48, 157) clearly imply a first-hand account by a member of the senatorial elite.

92 **Tyrannicide.** See on 63 above.

'Friend, ...' Odysseus to Agamemnon (*Iliad* XIV 90–1), 'slightly misquoted.

94 **I notice.** Text uncertain. A comment by J., or taken from his source?

Mime. Catullus' *Laureolus* (Suet. *Cal.* 57.4) on which see T.P. Wiseman, *Catullus and his World* (Cambridge 1985) 258f, and V. Schmidt, *Latomus* 42 (1983) 156–60.

Leader. Evidently of a group of bandits (cf. Martial *De spectaculis* 7).

Dancer. I.e. Mnester (Suet. *Cal.* 57.4), the greatest star of his day;

sexual partner of Gaius (Suet. *Cal.* 36.1, 55.1), as later of Messallina (Dio LX 22.3–5, 28.3) and Poppaea Sabina (Tac. *Ann.* IX 4.1); executed by Claudius in 48 (Tac. *Ann.* XI 36). For the tragic ballet of the *pantomimi*, see Lucian's essay *The Dance* (in volume 5 of the Loeb translation).

Cinyras. Founder of Paphos in Cyprus, and unwitting father of his daughter's child Adonis; the story of Myrrha's passion and fate is in Ovid *Metamorphoses* X 298–552. According to Suetonius (*Cal.* 57.4), the same tragedy had been performed at the theatrical festival in 336 when Philip II of Macedon was assassinated (cf. 95 below).

Both killed. Cinyras committed suicide; but Myrrha was metamorphosed into a tree. J. may have misunderstood the nature of the omen: not blood, as in the *Laureolus*, but the choice of the play itself?

95   **Date.** Another misunderstanding? The assassination of Philip took place in the summer (see N.G.L. Hammond and G.T. Griffith, *History of Macedonia* 2 [Oxford 1979] 680–4). The emphasis on the Philip parallel may be due to flatterers of Claudius: the king assassinated at the theatre was succeeded by Alexander the Great.

96   **Gaius was wondering.** There had been a great banquet the day before, and Gaius was not sure whether his digestion could cope with lunch (Suet. *Cal.* 58.1).

Bathe. Unfortunately for our understanding of the topography (103–4 below) the location of the baths in the imperial complex is unknown.

Minucianus. I.e. Vinicianus (see on 18 above).

97   **The emperor.** Literally 'Caesar' (see on 75 above).

98   **Asprenas.** The MSS have 'Ambronas' or 'Ampronas', an impossible name; one MS has 'Asprinas' in the margin, the sixth-century Latin translation has 'Aspronas', and the tenth-century epitomator gives 'Asprenas', which has a good chance of being right. See 87 above: a man close enough to get splashed by the emperor's sacrifice will have been sitting close enough to talk to him now (Jung 379 n. 45).

99–113   The deed is done. Suetonius (*Cal.* 58) gives two versions of the assassination, both different from J.'s in the details. (Momigliano 808 assumes that J.'s source gave one of Suetonius' versions, but the divergences noted at 99, 104, 105 and 109 below make that very unlikely.) The author of J.'s main source was evidently stuck in the theatre at the time (see on 91 above), so there is no need to privilege his account.

99 **Mid-afternoon.** Literally the ninth hour (from dawn); Suetonius (*Cal.* 58.1) says the seventh.

100 **Made Chaerea resolve.** Timpe (*RG* 495) unnecessarily doubts the authenticity of this 'unfulfilled intention'. But he is right to stress its exemplary force as evidence for Chaerea's uncompromising priorities.

Knights. No doubt particularly the Praetorian Prefects: see on 37 above.

Liberty. See on 42 above.

101 **Out of the way.** So also in one of the Suetonius versions, the crowd was moved back 'by centurions who were in the plot' (*Cal.* 58.2) on the excuse that the emperor wanted privacy (*Claud.* 10.1).

102 **First to come out.** Interpreted by Levick (35)—implausibly, I think— as 'an act of surprising discourtesy' and therefore evidence for the three men's complicity in the plot. There is no sign that J.'s source was surprised.

Claudius. Confirmed by Dio (LX 1.3).

Marcus Vinicius. Consul in 30, married Julia Livilla soon after 33 (Tac. *Ann.* VI 15.1); 'an elegant orator and gentle in disposition ... a man of unobtrusive virtue' (Syme *AA* 173, 278). Velleius Paterculus dedicated his history to him as consul (A.J. Woodman, *Classical Quarterly* 25 [1975] 273–5). See further 251 below.

Valerius Asiaticus. I.e. D. Valerius Asiaticus of Vienne (Narbonensis), suffect consul in 35, owner of the sumptuous Gardens of Lucullus on the Pincio (Tac. *Ann.* XI 1); 'his was a courage and dignity that most of the aristocracy had forfeited—and a splendour of living that surpassed them' (Syme *Tac.* 579); husband of Lollia Saturnina, whose sexual performance Gaius criticised in Asiaticus' presence (Sen. *Const.* 18.2). See further 159 and 252 below.

Paullus Arruntius. Not otherwise known. Conjectured by Syme (*AA* 262f, 268f, stemma XV) to be a son of the L. Arruntius whom Augustus judged capable of ruling (Tac. *Ann.* I 13), and therefore brother by adoption of the L. Arruntius Camillus Scribonianus who with Annius Vinicianus rebelled against Claudius in 42 (Dio LX 15.1–2). The name 'Paullus' is attested only in the Latin version. Bernard Kavanagh, *Latomus* 69 (2010) 1007–17, suggests the emendation 'Aquila', and identifies this man with the Aquila who gave Gaius the death-blow (110 below) and with Marcus Aquila Iulianus the consul of 38, who was evidently an Arruntius.

103   **Inside the residence.**   Presumably via the portico (90 above).

Direct routes.   Literally 'roads' or 'streets', as at 116–17 and 212 below; the imperial property consisted of separate houses (117 below), presumably with streets and alleys between them.

104   **Empty alleyway.**   The same word (*stenopos*) is used at Dio LIX 29.6, and is consistent with 'narrow streets' at 116 below. Suetonius, on the other hand, whose account of the assassination differs from J.'s in various ways (see K. Scherberich, *Rheinisches Museum* 142 [1999] 74–83), says that the boys were rehearsing in a *crypta*, presumably a basement area rather than merely a covered passage (Suet. *Cal.* 58.1). See Appendix 1: the two accounts may not be irreconcilable.

Boys from Asia.   According to Dio (LIX 29.6), they were boys of good family from Greece and Ionia who had been summoned to sing the hymn to Gaius. Suetonius (*Cal.* 58.1) reports that Gaius stopped to talk to them, and would have gone back to have their performance put on straight away if the choir leader had not complained of cold.

Mysteries. See on 30 and 77 above.

Pyrrhic dances.   Originally the frenetic armed dance of the Cretan Curetes or Corybantes, the *pyrrhicha* by the first century AD had evidently become a spectacular mythological ballet (Suet. *Nero* 22.2, Apuleius *Metamorphoses* X 29–34: Pasiphae, Icarus, judgement of Paris), frequently involving performing animals (Pliny *NH* VIII 5, Babrius 80: elephants, camel).

At the theatres.   They eventually gave one performance; Claudius rewarded them with Roman citizenship and sent them home (Dio LX 7.2).

105   **Asked for the password.**   See on 29 and 31 above. Contrast Suet. *Cal.* 58.2, where Chaerea is standing *behind* Gaius; one of Suetonius' versions implies, and the other states explicitly, that Cornelius Sabinus asked for the password. No doubt J.'s source wanted to intensify the dramatic irony.

With a curse.   Contrast Suet. *Cal.* 58.2, where Chaerea's exclamation has a ritual significance. In Suetonius' first version he shouts 'Hoc age!', the formula for the attendant at a sacrifice to kill the victim; he then strikes Gaius on the neck with his sword, while Sabinus, facing the emperor, stabs him through the chest. In Suetonius' second version, Sabinus asks for the password and is given 'Jupiter'; Chaerea shouts 'Accipe ratum!' (for which Barrett 165 suggests 'accept the fulfilment of your vow'), and when Gaius looks round breaks his jawbone with a cut of his sword. According to Seneca (*Const.* 18.3), Chaerea cut through Gaius' neck with one blow, but whether from the front (as in J.) or from behind (as in Suetonius' version 1) is not made clear.

106   **I know there are some.**   Cf. 68 above. 106–8, arguably the most ill-timed digression in the history of narrative, is surely J.'s own contribution; his source probably did attribute this motive to Chaerea, for the sake of dramatic irony (cf. 105 above) and to explain why his hero did not deliver the *coup de grace* (111 below).

   Wounding him many times.   'There was a tradition, preserved in Suetonius, of Gaius liking to watch a lingering death . . . and therefore some writer (we cannot say who) gratified his moral sense by imagining that Gaius in the end met the same agonising death that he was supposed to love inflicting on others' (Charlesworth 112, on Suet. *Cal.* 30.1). I think we *can* say who: J.'s own source, whose interpretation he could not accept.

107   **Vengeance.**   At the hands of the Germans (12.1–6, 150f, 215), or by arrest and trial (cf. 158, 218).

108   **The opportunity.**   Cf. 27 above.

   Anyone who wants to.   Cf. 196 below. A favourite formula of J.'s: *Ant.* I 108, II 348, III 81, 268, 322, IV 158, VIII 262.

109   **Did not shout.**   Contrast Suet. *Cal.* 58.3, where Gaius calls out that he is still alive, and his litter-bearers come to his aid.

110   **Cornelius Sabinus.**   See on 46 and 105 above.

   Several of them.   Thirty, according to Suetonius (*Cal.* 58.3, who adds that some aimed at his genitals; Gaius' predatory sexual behaviour had invited that sort of revenge (Dio LIX 28.9, Suet. *Cal.* 36, 41.1), and Seneca (*Const.* 18.3) specified that the vengeance was 'for public *and private* wrongs'. According to Dio (LIX 29.7), 'some even tasted of his flesh'.

   Aquila.   See on 102 above: the identification with the consul of 38 is suggested also by Galimberti (183–4). But one would expect J. to have mentioned the involvement of such a senior senator at this dramatic moment.

Without dispute. Implying there *was* a dispute about the heroism of Chaerea himself. See on 46 and 105 above for versions which gave Sabinus at least an equal status, and on 106 above for the special pleading of J.'s source.

111   **Should have the credit.** Seneca (*Const.* 18.3) agrees: 'Chaerea was the first among the conspirators to lift his hand.' Scherberich (150–1) assumes that J.'s main source was a monograph like Sallust's *Catiline*, focussing specifically on Chaerea. But that is an unnecessary hypothesis: a historian like Cluvius Rufus might equally well have chosen to structure this part of his narrative around one particular protagonist.

112   **First had the courage.** See 32 and 37.
        Gathered together. See 46–9.
        Good speeches. See 78–83.

113   **Initiative.** See 100.
        Seized the honour. See 105.

114–26 The conspirators escape, and the German bodyguards look for vengeance.

114   **Such was the end.** For this commonplace, see H. MacL. Currie, *Latomus* 48 (1989) 346–53. He calls it 'an obituary formula in the historians', and it is indeed frequent in obituary passages: e.g. Velleius II 72.1 (Brutus), Curtius Rufus VII 2.33 (Parmenion), and above all Tac. *Hist.* I 49 (Galba); see on 201 below. But here and at 272 below it is used as a passing comment of irony or pathos, and most of Currie's examples are of this type. The earliest use of it known to me is Herodotus V 48 on Dorieus; the latest, Syme *AA* 108 ('Such was the end of M. Lepidus …').

115   **The foolish people.** See 158f and 228 below; and compare Tac. *Hist.* I 4 on Nero and the *plebs sordida*.

116   **Streets.** See on 104 above.
        Crowd. See on 101 above.
        Servants. Including those who lined the route at 103 above.
        On duty. Chaerea's cohort, or Sabinus'? See on 31 and 105 above.

117   **House of Germanicus.** Site unknown. Henry Hurst's argument in *Lexicon Topographicum Urbis Romae* II (1995) 111–12, that it might be below the north-west corner of the Palatine behind the temple of Castor and Pollux, depends on 'an association of this area with the

name Germanicus, which survives later in the reference to *horrea Germaniciana et Agrippiana* in the Regionary Catalogues'. But those *horrea* (granaries) were more probably named after Germanicus' father Nero Drusus Germanicus (Wiseman *Pal.* 249). In any case, there is no reason to suppose that the assassins escaped in the direction of the Forum; Chaerea, at least, rejoined his cohort (153 below). Wherever they went, their first preoccupation must have been to wash off the bloodstains.

Made up severally.   Remains of a few of these separate houses survive: the 'Casa dei Grifi' and the 'Aula Isiaca', below the Lararium and Basilica (respectively) of the Flavian palace, and the 'Cryptoporticus' in the foundations of the Domus Tiberiana beneath the Farnese Gardens. For the latter, see Maria Antonietta Tomei and Maria Grazia Filetici, *Domus Tiberiana scavi e restauri 1990–2011* (Milan 2011) 206–39.

Named after those who had built them.   The 'house of Hortensius' and the 'house of Catulus' (Suet. *Augustus* 72.1, *De grammaticis* 17.2) were parts of Augustus' original complex; the 'house of Tiberius' (Suet. *Vitellius* 15.3, Plutarch *Galba* 24.4 etc) is attested only in its post-Neronian form.

119   **The first people.**   Contrast Suet. *Cal.* 58.3: Gaius' litter-bearers first, then (*mox*) the Germans.

German bodyguard.   See Millar 62f: a corps of Batavian cavalry (Dio LV 24.7), employed by Augustus as bodyguards from 30 BC to AD 9 (Suet. *Augustus* 49.1), and again by Tiberius and his successors (Tac. *Ann.* I 24.2, XIII 18.3, XV 58.2), but disbanded by Galba in 68 (Suet. *Galba* 12.2).

Celtic nation.   Posidonius, the earliest classical author to deal with the Germans, evidently did not distinguish them from the Celts (I.G. Kidd, *Posidonius: the Commentary* [Cambridge 1988] 323–6). According to Caesar (*Gallic War* I 1.3), the Rhine was the ethnic boundary; but that was an oversimplification (C.M. Wells, *The German Policy of Augustus* [Oxford 1972] 14–31).

120   **National characteristic.**   Cf. Diodorus V 29 (on the Gauls, from Posidonius), Caesar *Gallic War* VI 23f, Tacitus *Germania* 14.

122   **Sabinus.**   According to Suetonius (*Cal.* 55.2), Gaius put Thracian gladiators in charge of his German bodyguard. J.'s source no doubt drew attention to Sabinus (not to be confused with Cornelius Sabinus

the conspirator) because he was later one of the lovers of Claudius'
empress Messallina (Dio LX 28.2).

Through the house. J. uses 'the house' and 'the residence'
interchangeably (*oikos* or *oikia* at 122, 126, 162 and 212, *basileion* at 75,
103 and 195), no doubt reproducing *domus* and *Palatium* (respectively)
in his Latin source. After Nero, when practically all the Palatine was
imperial property, *Palatium* could be used in the sense of 'the palace',
though only anachronistically in a narrative of AD 41.

123   **Asprenas.** See on 87 and 98 above: was he one of the conspirators? If
so, the Germans got it right by accident. Suetonius (*Cal.* 58.3) describes
all the senators they killed as 'innocent'.

Norbanus Balbus. If we accept the emendation *Balbos* for *Barbaros,*
he was probably either L. Norbanus Balbus, consul in 19 (and so now
in his middle to late fifties), or a son of the same name. Barrett (162)
and Ferrill (161) assume he was in the plot, but the narrative gives us
no reason to think so.

Noblest. Cf. 52 on Vinicianus. Slightly overstated, though there had
been three earlier generations of consular Norbani (in 83, 38 and
24 BC). Perhaps J.'s source was flattering a still powerful family: a
Norbanus was Praetorian Prefect in the last years of Domitian (Dio
LXVII 15.2).

Many generals. One is known from the *Fasti triumphales*: the consul
of 38 BC held a triumph for his campaigns in Spain.

125   **Anteius.** Not otherwise known. No doubt related to P. Anteius Rufus
the friend of Agrippina, who committed suicide in 66 (Tac. *Ann.* XVI
14), and to Anteia the wife of the younger Helvidius Priscus (Pliny
Letters IX 13.4).

His father. Perhaps the Anteius who had served under Germanicus
in 16 (Tac. *Ann.* II 6.1).

To kill him. On Gaius' order to execute exiles, see Suet. *Cal.* 28, Dio
LIX 18.3, Orosius VII 5.9.

127–37   Reaction in the theatre. Clearly a first-hand description (see on 91
above), and one which vividly evokes the senatorial elite's fear and
loathing of Gaius.

129   **Children.** So J. says: but 'the younger generation' (*to neoteron*) at 130
below suggests that his source had a more general term (e.g. *iuventus*).

The implication is that the young people, like the women and slaves, were mindlessly irresponsible.

Reluctant to accept. Cf. Suet. *Cal.* 60: people thought it was a rumour made up by Gaius himself to test reaction. See Barrett 229 on Gaius' popularity.

The soldiers' attitude. Compare Tacitus' classic description of the Praetorians in 69 (Tac. *Hist.* I 5, 18, 46).

130   **Popular delights.** Cf. Tac. *Hist.* I 4, where Tacitus attributes similar motives to the *plebs sordida* in 69: 'the riff-raff haunting the circus and theatres, and the scum of the slave population, or those spendthrifts and bankrupts who had been the recipients of Nero's degrading charity' (trans. K. Wellesley). But J.'s Thucydidean phrase (Thuc. II 65.4 etc) also conveys the idea of the fickleness of the crowd.

Gladiatorial shows. Literally 'gifts', J.'s translation of *munera* in his Latin source.

Welfare of the people. Cf. Suet. *Cal.* 17.2, 18.2, Dio LIX 7.1, 13.9: feasts for the populace.

Bloodthirsty. Cf. Suet. *Cal.* 27–32 on Gaius' *saevitia*; but Gaius' fondness for huge sacrifices is more relevant to his extravagance (Suet. *Cal.* 37).

Madness. See on 1 above.

131   **Slaves.** See 12 and 14 above: the same point, taken from a different source.

Informers. At his accession, Gaius announced that unlike Tiberius he would not listen to informers (Suet. *Cal.* 15.4, cf. Dio LIX 4.3); but that policy was soon reversed (Suet. *Cal.* 30.2, Dio LIX 16.8).

One eighth. It was a quarter under the Augustan treason law (Tac. *Ann.* IV 20.2), and more than that under the *lex Papia Poppaea* (Suet. *Nero* 10.1); but those were rewards for prosecutors—usually senators—and not for slaves who merely provided evidence.

132   **The aristocrats.** J.'s word *eupatridai* normally means 'patricians', but here (and at 136 and *Bell.* II 212) it probably translates a more general word or phrase in his source—e.g. *patres* (senators) or *optimus quisque*. The description of the pathology of tyranny in 132–7 is reminiscent of Tacitus (e.g. *Agr.* 2.3, 45.2, *Ann.* IV 69f, VI 7.3); see Wirszubski 164f.

133   **Dared not speak.** Cf. Tac. *Ann.* XI 34.1, on L. Vitellius and Caecina Largus in 48.

134   **Rival story.** See on 128 above (Suet. *Cal.* 60).

      Doctors. See on 237 below (Agrippa's story).

136   **Haranguing the people.** Certainly the people were indignant (158–9 below), and Gaius would have found it easy to whip them up against the Senate (228 below).

137   **Prosecutors and judges.** I.e. in a treason trial, if Gaius was not dead after all.

138–57 A massacre is narrowly averted. This continuation of the scene in the theatre contains two rhetorical set-pieces: the pathetic pleas at 139–41 and Clemens' speech at 155–6. But they are handled with commendable brevity, and subordinated to the authentic detail of the first-hand narrative (which secures an honourable place in history for Alcyon the doctor and Evarestus the auctioneer).

141   **Calling on the gods.** J.'s word *epitheiazontes* is Thucydidean (Thuc. II 75.1, VIII 35.2, cf. VII 75.1).

142   **It was brutal ...** For a very similar comment (of the mutineers in AD 14), see Tac. *Ann.* I 35.

      Asprenas and the others. See 123–6 above.

      On the altar. See 87 above.

144   **Deprived of all pleasure and joy.** Text uncertain: the MSS have 'deprived of the place of pleasures', which is meaningless.

145   **Arruntius Evarestus.** Probably a freedman, to judge by the Greek *cognomen*; Arruntius Stella (148 below) may have been his patron. For auctioneers, their business and their social status in the first century AD, see J. Andreau, *Les affaires de Monsieur Jucundus* (Rome 1974). On this occasion, his voice will have mattered most.

      Equal to the richest. For wealthy freedmen (cf. 64 above), see Pliny *NH* XXXIII 134–5, with Susan Treggiari, *Roman Freedmen during the Late Republic* (Oxford 1969) 239f, and J.H. D'Arms, *Commerce and Social Standing in Ancient Rome* (Harvard 1981) 97–120.

147   **Proceeded.** From where? How had he heard the news?

148   **Arruntius Stella.** Certainly related to, and perhaps identical with, L. Arruntius Stella the organiser of Nero's games in 55 (Tac. *Ann.* XIII 22.1), whose grandson was consul in 101, 'high-born and wealthy ... gifted, eloquent and poetical' (Syme *Tac.* 88: Statius *Silvae* I 2.71 for his patrician birth); there was probably a Flavian consul in the intervening

generation. Feldman (283 n. *a*) emends away Stella's *cognomen* in this passage, and attributes his action to Evarestus, but a mere auctioneer would have no authority over the Germans. Though J. does not say so (no doubt over-abbreviating his source), it is possible that Stella was the other Praetorian Prefect (see on 37 above).

Tribunes.   I.e. colleagues of Chaerea and Cornelius Sabinus (see on 18 above). Officers commanding the Praetorian cohorts naturally outranked Sabinus and his fellow-gladiators (122 above).

149   **It is very clear.**   The authoritative judgement of an eye-witness.

151   **Where authority would lie.**   The constitutionally proper order of alternatives: see Wiseman *KC* 4–5 on the theoretical dispensability of the *princeps*.

Whoever else.   The male line of the Iulii Caesares ended with Gaius, and he had put his designated heir to death (M. Lepidus, see on 20 above). So if there was to be a new *princeps*, it was not obvious who it would be.

153   **Chaerea.**   The first mention of him since the escape of the assassins at 117 above. J. doesn't say (because his source didn't know?) where Chaerea now was.

Minucianus.   I.e. Vinicianus (see on 18 above).

The soldiers.   Presumably his own cohort, though it is not clear where they were stationed (see on 105 and 116 above).

154   **Brought before Clemens.**   As Timpe suggests (*UK* 83), this was probably the official enquiry into the murder, referred to at 158 below. But his idea that it took place in the theatre is surely impossible: if Clemens had been in the theatre, he would have been mentioned at 148. The whole passage, as Timpe observes, is an interpolation into the theatre scene. 'This account, which stresses the great perils to which Vinicianus was supposedly exposed, may cover the reality that he, in fact, sought Clemens' protection at the first sign of danger' (Barrett 166). Perhaps; but on the question of Clemens' sympathies (see below) it is impossible to penetrate beyond J.'s source to the historical reality.

Testifying to the courage.   Clemens' noble speech is clearly the *raison d'être* of the whole episode. J.'s source was no doubt influenced by the fact that Clemens' son was a distinguished Flavian senator (consul in 73 and again probably in 85), and his daughter the first wife of Vespasian's elder son (Suet. *Titus* 4.2).

155   **Pleasure of outrageous violence.** *Hybris,* violence and self-indulgence
       were all characteristics of the tyrant (see the classic description in Plato
       Republic IX 572d–575d).
       Virtue hates him. See on 171 below; and cf. Tac. *Ann.* XVI 21.1
       ('virtutem ipsam excindere') on Nero's destruction of Thrasea and
       Soranus.

156   **Conspirator against himself.** The defence of justifiable tyrannicide
       was familiar in Rome long before the Ides of March (e.g. Cicero *Pro
       Milone* 80–3); see Wiseman *KC* 5–8. But the idea that the tyrant kills
       himself is a rhetorical conceit.
       Care for the law. See on 15 above.
       Even his friends. So too 211 below (the obituary).

157   **Alcyon.** No doubt identical with 'Alcon the wound-surgeon',
       mentioned by the elder Pliny (*NH* XXIX 22) in the context of high
       medical fees.
       Was seized. By whom? Presumably the Germans, on whom Norbanus
       Balbus (124 above) may have inflicted some casualties.

158–66 The Senate and People of Rome resume responsibility. Doublets
        (160/189) and inconsistencies (158f/189) indicate that J. has spliced
        together at least two sources for this part of the story: 158–60 and
        160–89 probably represent two versions of the same debate. Most of
        the Senate's deliberations have been omitted (see on 160); Timpe (*RG*
        477–8) attributes that to the artistic selectivity of J.'s main source.

158   **The Senate was in session.** Where? 'The Senate was so unanimously
       in favour of re-establishing the Republic that the consuls called the first
       meeting not in the Senate-house, because it bore the name Julia, but
       in the Capitol' (Suet. *Cal.* 60); so too Dio LX 1.1, and J. himself at *Bell.*
       II 205. But in this work J. implies that the Senate was convened on the
       Capitol only later (see on 248 below). If its first business was indeed
       an enquiry into the murder, the consuls were no doubt being cautious;
       the symbolic move to the Capitol (cf. Talbert 116–17) will have followed
       after the members' attitudes became clear.
       The people were assembled. J.'s phraseology seems to imply a
       proper meeting (*contio,* cf. Tac. *Ann.* XI 1.2) under the presidency
       of a magistrate, which is not impossible. The popular assemblies
       did still meet, for formal legislation (the last known *lex* is dated AD

97: *Digest* XLVII 21.3.1) and for ratifying the election of magistrates (Dio LVIII 20.4, Pliny *Panegyricus* 63.2, 92.4); Gaius had even briefly restored to them the elections themselves (Dio LIX 9.6, 20.3f, Suet. *Cal.* 16.2). Moreover, expressions of popular opinion—on the recall of Julia (Dio LV 13.1), Claudius' marriage (Tac. *Ann.* XII 7.1), the recognition of Galba (Plutarch *Galba* 7.2)—may have resulted from formal *contiones* rather than mere haphazard shouting.

The customary place. A comment for non-Roman readers, as at 3 (*equites*), 4 (Capitol), 24 (*ludi circenses*), 202 (Praetorians).

Went about it eagerly. For popular loyalty to Gaius and the Principate, see 115, 136, 227f (also Suet. *Claud.* 10.4, Dio LIX 30.3); on the other hand, at 189, 191 and 272 J. reports popular sympathy for the tyrannicides. We should probably infer two sources with inconsistent views.

159 **Valerius Asiaticus.** See on 102 above. According to the epitomator of Dio (LIX 30.2), his heroic declaration was delivered to the Praetorian Guard. The report of it may not be unconnected with the prominence of his descendants: M. Lollius Paullinus D. Valerius Asiaticus Saturninus was twice consul (94, 125) and Prefect of the City. When Asiaticus was tried for treason in 47, it was alleged that he had been a ringleader in the conspiracy against Gaius (Tac. *Ann.* XI 1); Ferrill 161 assumes that was true, but it is clearly inconsistent with J.'s account.

160 **The consuls.** I.e. Cn. Sentius Saturninus and Q. Pomponius Secundus. Sentius was the grandson of C. Sentius Saturninus, who as consul in 19 BC, while Augustus was away, had exercised his authority with old-fashioned energy and rigour (Velleius II 92); for his family, see R. Syme, *Roman Papers* (Oxford 1979) 605–16. He is named along with Thrasea Paetus and Barea Soranus as one of the victims of Nero's last years (Tac. *Hist.* IV 7). Pomponius, who was responsible for summoning the Senate (263 below), was half-brother to Caesonia, Gaius' empress (Pliny *NH* VII 39, with Syme, *Roman Papers* 805–14); he joined the rebellion of Arruntius Scribonianus in 42, and either committed suicide or was executed (Tac. *Ann.* XIII 43.2).

Put out an edict. J. has omitted a great deal here. The consuls mobilised the urban cohorts to secure the Forum and Capitol (Suet. *Claud.* 10.3, J. *Bell.* II 205); summoned the Senate to the Capitol (see on 158 above); sent a stern message to Claudius (see on 229–36 below); transferred the public treasury, under the guard of the urban cohorts, from the temple of Saturn to the Capitol (Dio LIX 30.3); and presided over a debate in which it was resolved to wipe out the entire family of the Caesars and all their relatives, women included, and to destroy the temples of Divus Iulius and Divus Augustus (Orosius VII 6.3, Vict. *Caes.* 3.16, Suet. *Cal.* 60). The edict J. refers to here must have been issued at the *end* of that debate.

Ordered the people. The withdrawal of the populace and the dismissal of the soldiers is reported (in the proper place) at 189 below. The doublet implies that J. has given a very compressed account of the Senate's debate from one source, followed by a longer one (though restricted almost entirely to Sentius' speech) from another.

The soldiers. Presumably the urban cohorts (Suet. *Claud.* 10.3, cf. 188 below and J. *Bell.* II 2.05). There were three cohorts, numbered in sequence with the nine of the Praetorian Guard; their pay was half that of the Praetorians, but 66% more than that of legionaries (Suet. *Augustus* 101.3). Their commander was probably the Prefect of the City (a senior senator appointed by the emperor), but it is clear that on this occasion the consuls assumed command.

Grievances. Cf. 25 above.

161   **By now.** Inconsistent with 160 above (the consuls' edict), and thus evidence of a change of source.

Full membership. That would be over 400 senators (Talbert 149–52); contrast 249 below.

Those who had joined the plot. 'These men [the consuls], together with the prefects and the followers of Sabinus and Chaerea, were deliberating what should be done' (Dio LIX 30.3).

High opinion of themselves. This unexpected description of the conspirators' demeanour (cf. 255 below) may be evidence of a first-hand narrative; if, as is likely, J.'s main source was a senator, he will have left the theatre at the first opportunity to obey the consuls' summons.

Depended on them. J.'s Greek could mean 'had been handed to them'.

162   **Claudius.** Last seen leaving the theatre at 102–3 above.

Kidnapped. The fuller account at 212–22 below is no doubt from a different source.

From the house. I.e. the imperial complex (see on 75, 104 and 117 above). Not 'from his house', as in Feldman (289).

Held a meeting. See 223–6 below.

A republic. Here, and at 173 and 187 below, J. uses *demokratia* for the Republic (contrast 224 on 'the Senate in power' and *Bell.* II 205 on *aristokratia*). It is the first extant example of a usage common in later Greek historians, particularly Appian and Dio: see G.E.M. De Ste Croix, *The Class Struggle in the Ancient Greek World* (London 1981) 322f, 614f.

In their interest. See 214, 225 below; cf. Tac. *Hist.* I 5, 25 etc. In a republic, the Praetorian Guard would have no reason to exist (cf. Dio LIII 11.5). As Timpe (*UK* 88) rightly points out, this reason for the soldiers' decision marks a turning-point in the theory of the Principate; in a real sense, Claudius was indeed 'the first Roman emperor' (C.E. Stevens, in Levick 41).

164 **Choose an emperor themselves.** Compare the Praetorian coup that put Otho in power (Tac. *Hist.* I 21–49).

Uncle. As the brother of Gaius' father Germanicus (see on 217 below). But though Germanicus was adopted into the Julian family (Tac. *Ann.* I 3.5, Suet. *Tiberius* 15.2), Claudius was not: he remained a Claudius Nero, not a Iulius Caesar.

More illustrious. J.'s other version of the Praetorians' reasoning (223 below) more plausibly emphasises the reputation of Germanicus and their distrust of the Senate. According to Dio (LX 1.3), they chose him 'because he was of the imperial family and was regarded as suitable'.

Distinction of his ancestors. The Claudii were an ancient patrician family (their first consulship was in 495 BC); the branch that used the *praenomen* Tiberius and the *cognomen* Nero was descended from one of the sons of Appius Claudius Caecus, censor in 312 BC (Suet. *Tiberius* 3.1).

Devotion to learning. See Suet. *Claud.* 3.1, 41–2, and 213 below. Literary studies, which were regarded as a training for good character (Noè 107, cf. Cicero *Pro Archia* 14), might be considered a proper qualification for an emperor (cf. 208–11 below), but hardly by the Praetorian Guard; the comment probably reflects the view of J.'s source.

165 **Reward them.** So too in the other version (225 below). And he did so (247 below).

It was carried out. In this version (contrast 214–25 below), they choose Claudius *before* they seize him.

166   **Gnaeus Sentius Saturninus.**   See on 160 above. Not identified by J. as
one of the consuls (contrast *Bell.* II 205); Timpe (*RG* 476 n. 8) suggests
that the title was mentioned earlier by J.'s source in a passage J. has
omitted, but the use of the full three names implies that this was his
formal introduction.

Undeterred by the news.   Timpe (*RG* 476–8, 486f) cites this passage
and the 'ring scene' at 185 below as evidence for J.'s source's ironical
attitude to Sentius' speech: the great statement of liberty is made in the
knowledge that the Principate will continue, and with the tyrant's own
image on the orator's hand. Noè (112) and Galimberti (189) agree. But
I think Timpe exaggerates; it was still far from clear that the Claudius
coup was going to succeed (cf. Suet. *Claud.* 10.3, and 238 below), and
the emphasis is on Sentius' determination.

Unwillingly, it appeared.   For Claudius' 'apparent' reluctance, cf. Dio
LX 1.3a.

167–84 The consul's speech. 'This uninhibited exercise of freedom in a free
society expresses the true longings of the republican opposition in
the Senate' (Timpe *RG* 485, cf. Wirszubski 124–9). Barrett (174) doubts
the sincerity of Sentius' republicanism, but cites no evidence for his
allegation that according to J., Sentius 'was really a candidate for the
principate himself'.

167   **Romans.**   A significant vocative: one would expect 'senators', but
evidently J.'s source did not make Sentius say *patres conscripti*. Cf. Tac.
Ann. IV 34.1: Cremutius Cordus in his history called Caesar's assassin
C. Cassius 'the last of the Romans' (and died for it, under Tiberius).

So long a time.   See on 187 below.

The gods.   For the gods' gift, cf. 219 below (Gratus to Claudius).

168   **Independent judgement.**   Text uncertain.

Enough to live.   For the phrase, cf. Tac. *Ann.* IV 39.4 (Sejanus to
Tiberius).

Laws.   See on 15 above.

169   **Born too late.**   Descended from two generations of Augustan consuls,
and himself *consul ordinarius* in 41, Sentius was no doubt born about
AD 7 (cf. Syme *Tac.* 653f).

These men.   The purpose of Sentius' speech is to propose honours for
the tyrannicides (182–4 below).

171   **Virtue.**   For *virtus* (*arete* in J.'s Greek) as the defining characteristic of the Roman republican tradition, see for instance Plautus *Amphitryo* 75f, Cicero *Verrines* IV 81, *Philippics* IV 13, Sallust *Catiline* 6.5, 7.5, 53.4; Donald Earl, *The Moral and Political Tradition of Rome* (London 1967), esp. ch. 1.

172   **Only from report.**   The antithesis of *akoe* (hearing) and *opsis* (sight) is from Thucydides I 73.2. The question of their relative merits as sources of information became a historiographical commonplace: see Polybius XII 27.1, with F.W. Walbank's commentary (Oxford 1967, p. 408f).

     Excellence.   Literally 'virtue' (*arete*); see on 171 above. For the traditional hostility of tyrants to good men, see for instance Euripides *Suppliants* 444–6, Sallust *Catiline* 7.2, Tac. *Agr.* 41.1 ('infensus virtutibus princeps'); A.J. Woodman, *Velleius Paterculus: The Caesarian and Augustan Narrative* (Cambridge 1983) 142f.

     Flattery and fear.   Cf. Tac. *Ann.* I 1.2, on historians 'frightened off by the rising tide of flattery' (*gliscens adulatio*).

     Caprice.   Cf. Cicero *Ad familiares* IX 16.3 on Caesar the dictator (letter to Papirius Paetus in July 46 BC, trans. D.R. Shackleton Bailey): 'All becomes uncertain when the path of legality has been forsaken … There is no guaranteeing the future of what depends on someone's else's wishes, not to say whims.'

173   **Julius Caesar.**   He was said to have described the Republic as 'a mere name without body or form' (Titus Ampius, quoted in Suet. *Iulius* 77); for his approximation to kingship see S. Weinstock, *Divus Iulius* (Oxford 1971) 270–6. His dictatorship was naturally seen by the *optimates* as a tyranny (e.g. Cicero *De officiis* II 23, III 82–5), but so too was his consulship in 59 BC (see on 187 below); details in Wirszubski 74–9, 87–91.

174   **His successors.**   I.e. the Caesares: Augustus, Caesar's son (by adoption); Tiberius, Caesar's grandson (after adoption by Augustus in AD 4); Gaius, Caesar's great-great-grandson and the last of his line. See Timpe *RG* 497: the Principate was seen as a family dynasty (Tac. *Hist.* I 16), and the Senate resolved to extirpate the family (Suet. *Cal.* 60, Vict. *Caes.* 3.16, Orosius VII 6.3).

     Ancestral tradition.   I.e. freedom, which was synonymous with the Republic (Wirszubski 5, cf. 136–8 for the liberty of the Senate).

        Those with a reputation. See on 172 above.

175   **Indiscriminate.** Literally 'uneducated'.

        Relatives and friends. See on 20 above.

        Unjust revenge. Tiberius was particularly vindictive (Syme *Tac.* 423f).

176   **Outrageous pleasure.** See on 155 above.

        Assaults on property. Examples in Suet. *Cal.* 38–9.

        Wives. See on 110 above.

177   **All freedom is hateful.** See Tac. *Agr.* 3.1 on *libertas* as incompatible with *principatus*.

        His own deeds. J.'s text refers to tyrants in the plural. All these observations apply in general as well as to the particular case of Gaius.

178   **It is your duty.** Text uncertain.

        Declare your opinion against. A Thucydidean verb (*antapophainein*, Thuc. III 38.2, 67.3). For the sentiment, contrast Tac. *Ann.* I 74.5, a senior senator's reaction to a vote in the Senate: 'Caesar, will you vote first or last? If first, I shall have a lead to follow; if last, I'm afraid I may inadvertently disagree with you.'

180   **Nothing other than inaction.** What Tacitus called *patientia* (*Agr.* 2.3, *Ann.* III 65.3), or *segnitia* (*Hist.* I 88). For a good example, see Dio LIX 16.8–11 (Noè 116).

        Refusal to speak up. Cf. Tac. *Agr.* 45.1f for senatorial self-criticism.

181   **The pleasure of peace.** Another Thucydidean reminiscence (Thuc. I 120.3f)? Cf. Sallust *Histories* I fr. 55.25 (Lepidus' speech, on *otium cum servitio*), Tac. *Agr.* 3.1 (*inertiae dulcedo*), *Ann.* I 2.1 (*dulcedo otii*). See in general Wirszubski 91–6.

        Like slaves. So also at 227 below. Cf. Dio XLVI 32.1, 34.4, L 1.2 for the loss of republican liberty as 'slavery'. *Servitium* in this sense is a recurring theme of Tacitus' *Annals* (e.g. I 2.1, 7.1, 81.2); Charlesworth (117f) suggests that J.'s source influenced Tacitus.

182   **Our first duty.** As always, J.'s main source concentrates on Chaerea; for what he has left out, see on 160 above, 190 below.

        Honours. Cf. Cicero *Pro Milone* 80: the Romans were familiar with the Greek tradition of honouring tyrannicides. The proposal in March 44 BC to honour the assassins of Caesar, which was blocked by Antony, was made by Ti. Claudius Nero (Suet. *Tiberius* 4.1), the great-grandfather of Gaius himself.

In planning and action. As already emphasised at 111–13 above. For these two characteristics of the ideal leader, see Velleius II 79.2, with A.J. Woodman's commentary (Cambridge 1983, p. 199).

184 **Cassius and Brutus.** The memory of Caesar's assassins was a sensitive issue throughout the first century AD: cf. Tac. *Ann.* III 76 (funeral of Brutus' sister), IV 34–5 (Cremutius Cordus, see on 167 above), XVI 7.2 (Cassius as 'leader of the cause'), Pliny *Letters* I 17.3. Gaius was warned to 'beware of Cassius' (Suet. *Cal.* 57.3). See Elizabeth Rawson in *Roman Culture and Society: Collected Papers* (Oxford 1991) 488–507. In the spring of 68, when Galba rebelled against Nero as 'legate of the Senate and People of Rome' (Suet. *Galba* 10.1), he struck *denarii* imitating Brutus' 'Ides of March' type of 43 BC, with daggers and cap of liberty: see M.H. Crawford, *Roman Republican Coinage* (Cambridge 1974) plate 61.19, and C.H.V. Sutherland, *Roman Imperial Coinage* I (second ed., London 1984) plate 23.24 = Smallwood no. 72(b).

Gaius Julius. Before the reign of Gaius, Caesar the dictator was referred to as 'C. Caesar' (e.g. Sallust *Catiline* 49.1, Velleius II 41.1, Valerius Maximus VI 6.15), which was the normal republican style for an aristocrat (see J.N. Adams, *Classical Quarterly* 28 [1978] 151–4 for Ciceronian conventions). The form 'C. Iulius', though not unknown in Cicero (*De provinciis consularibus* 39), is anomalous; its use here, and at Tac. *Hist.* I 50, may be to avoid confusion with 'C. Caesar' = Gaius Caligula (Tac. *Ann.* I 32.2, IV 71.1 etc).

Civil war. The implied contrast ('Chaerea's act has not brought civil war') is inconsistent with J.'s version at *Bell.* II 205, where the Senate, presumably at this meeting, declares war on Claudius; cf. also 2.41–3 below. No doubt J.'s source here was influenced by memories of the civil wars of 68 and 69 (Timpe *RG* 499).

185–9 The conclusion of the first meeting of the free Senate.

185 **Knights who were present.** The prefects (Dio LIX 30.3), and no doubt the non-senatorial conspirators (169 above, 'these men'), including Chaerea.

Trebellius Maximus. I.e. presumably M. Trebellius Maximus, legionary legate in Syria in 36 (Tac. *Ann.* VI 41.1), suffect consul with Seneca in 56, and imperial legate in Britain from 63 to 69 (Tac. *Agr.* 16, *Hist.* I 60): see A.R. Birley, *The Roman Government of Britain* (Oxford

2005) 52–6. Despite his inglorious record in Britain, he was *magister* of the Arval brethren in 72, and his survival and status under Vespasian doubtless accounts for the inclusion of this anecdote by J.'s source. Timpe (*RG* 491) infers from J.'s 'a certain (*tis*) Trebellius Maximus' that the source was being malicious; but the *tis* is probably J.'s own contribution.

Portrait of Gaius.   For Timpe's view of the significance of this episode (*RG* 476f, 486), see on 166 above.

186   **Night.**   See on 239 below.

'Liberty'.   See 54 above (Chaerea and Vinicianus).

Solemn act.   J.'s phrase (*to dromenon*) implies a dramatic ritual.

187   **Military commanders.**   A rhetorical over-simplification: in the late Republic it was rare for a consul to command troops during his year of office. But Timpe (*RG* 487) goes too far in inferring that the Senate had no real idea of what the Republic was like.

The hundredth year.   Counting from Caesar's first consulship in 59 BC—or perhaps the formation of the 'first triumvirate' in 60 BC, which is where Asinius Pollio began his history of the civil wars (Horace *Odes* II 1.1–8, cf. Syme *Tac.* 142 on Livy). See Noè 119 on the attempt by the historians of the early empire to identify the origins of the Principate: Tacitus (*Hist.* I 1) chose the battle of Actium as the crucial moment, but his contemporary Suetonius began with Caesar the dictator, evidently agreeing with J.'s main source (cf. 173–4 above). J. himself is inconsistent, making Augustus the first emperor at 75 above, but the second (and Gaius therefore the fourth) at *Ant.* XVIII 32 and 224. From the Senate's point of view, it was reasonable to pick on 59 BC in particular, since Cicero's letters of that year insisted that the Republic was totally lost (*Ad Quintum fratrem* I 2.15) and replaced by tyranny (*Ad Atticum* II 12.1, 13.2 etc; letter to Q. Axius quoted in Suet. *Julius* 9.2); see Wirszubski 75f.

Resumed the right.   An anachronism: there were no urban cohorts in the Republic for the consuls to give the password to.

188   **Four cohorts.**   Three, according to J. at *Bell.* II 205—presumably the three *cohortes urbanae* (Tac. *Ann.* IV 5, Suet. *Claud.* 10.3). J.'s figure here may be a mere copying error (reading IV for III in his Latin source?), since there is no likelihood that any of the Praetorian cohorts were loyal to the Republic.

189   **They marched off ... the people too.**   I.e., J. has now reached, with his main source, the events he has already reported at 160 above.

        Full of joy. See on 158 above. J.'s main source was evidently sanguine about popular enthusiasm for the Republic: his hero Chaerea had to be everybody's hero.

190–200 Gaius' wife and child are killed. The justification of the murder of Caesonia and little Julia Drusilla was evidently a sensitive question, both at the time and afterwards. What made it so was not just the brutality of the act (cf. Dio LVIII 11.5 for a comparable atrocity after the fall of Sejanus), but probably also the fact that Caesonia was (*a*) half-sister to the consul Q. Pomponius Secundus, and (*b*) the aunt of Domitia Longina, Domitian's empress at the time J. was writing. (For Caesonia's relatives, through her much-married mother Vistilia, see Pliny *NH* VII 39, with R. Syme, *Roman Papers* [Oxford 1979] 805–14.) J.'s anxiety to sit on the fence leads him to qualify his main source (friendly to Chaerea) with other versions.

190   **Meanwhile.**   For the problems created by J.'s chronology here, see Barrett 166f: 'the likelihood is that the murder of Caesonia had been decided upon well in advance ... and that it had been planned to follow almost immediately after Caligula's.' According to Vict. *Caes.* 3.16 (cf. Suet. *Cal.* 60, Orosius VII 6.3), the Senate at its first meeting resolved to wipe out the whole family of the Caesars, including the women ('etiam muliebri sexu'); that no doubt ratified a decision already taken by the conspirators.

        His whole family.   Cf. 221 and 258 below: Claudius to be taken before the consuls, or summarily executed.

        The rule of law.   See on 15 above. Caesonia might be pregnant again and produce a son; even her daughter could be a danger one day (cf. Tac. *Ann.* XIII 23.1 on Claudius' daughter Antonia).

        His hatred of Gaius.   The juxtaposition of the honourable with the less flattering motive may indicate that J. is already combining his main source with another version.

        One of the tribunes.   In Suetonius' version (*Cal.* 59) it is a centurion.

191   **Julius Lupus.**   Possibly father of Ti. Julius Lupus (Prefect of Egypt in 71) and grandfather of P. Julius Lupus (consul in 98). J.'s treatment of him is notably hostile (cf. 269 and 271 below).

Relative of Clemens. For a suggested reconstruction, making Lupus the brother of Clemens' wife, see Gavin Townend, *Journal of Roman Studies* 51 (1961) 57f and 62; modified by B.W. Jones, *The Emperor Titus* (London 1984) 19.

The reason. Levick (37f) is no doubt right to assume that the real motive was to implicate Clemens, but wrong to attribute that view to J. (see on 40 and 154 above).

The citizen body. See on 158 and 189 above: J.'s source at this point clearly assumes popular support for the tyrannicides.

192 **Some of the conspirators**. See on 190 above. The debate among the conspirators must have been during the planning period; any discussion at this stage would have been in the Senate.

Vent their anger on. Literally 'use boldness against', a curious phrase. 'Boldness' (*thrasos*) may translate the Latin *audacia*, in the sense of 'political criminality': see Ch. Wirszubski, *Journal of Roman Studies* 51 (1961) 12–22.

By his own nature. Cf. Suet. *Cal.* 11 on his cruel and vicious nature. 'It is not easy to distinguish the traits of character which Gaius inherited in the blood from those which he borrowed from the times ... he simply displayed in exaggerated form those weaknesses which were characteristic of the age in which he lived; he was prodigal, immoral, pleasure-loving, and cruel' (Balsdon 208, perhaps too indulgent).

193 **Others accused her**. See Suet. *Cal.* 50.2 and Juvenal VI 614–26 on the story of the drug and its effect—'fire and sword and torture, the blood of butchered knights and senators' (Juvenal).

Direct his passions. See Barrett 95f on Caesonia, Gaius' 'true soul-mate'; she was clearly a remarkable woman, and Gaius' devotion to her (Suet. *Cal.* 25.3, 33) made the story plausible. Noè (106) points out that Gaius' attack on the Senate dates from 39, the year of his marriage to Caesonia.

And their world empire. Cf. 1 and 14 above.

194 **For the good of the people**. See on 189 and 191 above. J. juxtaposes the honourable motive with the less flattering description of Lupus' eagerness (cf. 190 above on Chaerea).

195 **Residence**. See on 75 and 122 above for J.'s word *basileion*.

Nothing had been done. I.e., this was before Agrippa had reached the scene (237 below).

Only audible words. If authentic, they must have been reported by Lupus himself.

196 **At the time … nowadays.** See Noè 100f, who aptly compares Tac. *Ann.* III 19.2 (on the death of Germanicus) for controversy both at the time and subsequently. It is clear that the issue of Caesonia's murder was contentious not only for J.'s sources but also when he himself was writing. Perhaps it was connected with the posthumous reputation of her half-brother Corbulo, one of whose daughters married Annius Vinicianus' son, the other was Domitian's empress. 'In the end, Corbulo gets involved with enemies of the dynasty, or is incriminated through various ties or sympathies that united him to their company' (R. Syme, *Roman Studies* [Oxford 1979] 805–24, quotation from p. 824); Tacitus, of course, made a hero of him (Syme *Tac.* 492f, 579).

197 **Had had word.** See on 14 and 43 above.

199 **Showed his errand gave him pleasure.** Literally 'gave no sign that it did not …' Contrast Lupus' behaviour at 271 below.

The last act of the drama. A suitably theatrical image for a very histrionic scene: cf. Cicero *Ad Atticum* I 18.2 ('curtain up on the drama of Clodius'), Tac. *Hist.* III 83 (eye-witnesses like an applauding audience), Marcus Aurelius *Meditations* X 27 (history and experience like old plays revived). Cf. Timpe *RG* 479 on the juxtaposition of this scene with Gaius' obituary, which no doubt implies that the end of his rule came only with the extinction of his family.

200 **Killed her daughter.** According to Suetonius (*Cal.* 59), Caesonia was stabbed with a sword and the little girl smashed against a wall.

201–11 Gaius' obituary, 'a portrait which, while it recognised the evils of his reign, kept within the bounds of credibility and did not yield to sensationalism' (Charlesworth 118); as Timpe points out (*RG* 493), J.'s source is more moderate in his own assessment than in the speech he puts into the mouth of Sentius Saturninus. For obituary passages in historiography, see the elder Seneca, *Suasoria* 6.21 (trans. M. Winterbottom): 'This was done once or twice by Thucydides [e.g. II 65 on Pericles], and Sallust observed the practice in the case of a very few personages. The generous Livy bestowed it on all great men. Later historians have been much more lavish.' See R. Syme, *Ten Studies in Tacitus* (Oxford 1970) 79–90, on obituaries in Tacitus.

201 **Such was the end.** See on 114 above for the 'obituary formula'. Tacitus (*Ann.* VI 50.5) introduces his obituary of Tiberius with 'a phrase which, plain and majestic, stands unique in the literature of the Latins—"sic Tiberius finivit"' (Syme *Tac.* 342); contrast the usual 'hic exitus fuit' or 'hunc habuit finem'. J. has a similar verbal form here, but in Greek it is much less unusual.

Four years less four months. If Gaius was killed on 22 January (see on 77 and 85 above), the true figure is four years less 53 days; Tiberius died on 16 March 37.

Before he came to power. See on 192 above (innate viciousness), and 210 below (corrupted by power); Barrett (239) points out the inconsistency. Cf. Syme *Tac.* 436: 'Caligula possessed savage lucidity and a kind of frantic energy … Men could predict a cruel and capricious tyranny.'

Lover of malice. See Sen. *Const.* 18.1 for a contemporary's view.

Paralysed in the face of fear. Suetonius (*Cal.* 51) also notes the paradoxical combination of timorousness and confidence (with examples of the former).

Once he had his fill. See on 210 below.

Outrageous violence. I.e. *hybris*: see on 1 and 155 above.

Those who least deserved it. Actors, gladiators, ballplayers etc (Dio LIX 2.5, Macrobius *Saturnalia* II 6.5).

202 **Laws of gods and men.** J.'s phrase looks like a translation of *fas iusque* in his Latin source.

Flattery of the people. On Gaius' 'honeymoon period', see Suet. *Cal.* 13–14.

Punishment of virtue. See on 155 and 171 above.

203 **Punishment.** For Gaius' enjoyment of corporal and capital punishments, see Suet. *Cal.* 26–33.

No opposition. For Gaius' open expression of his own omnipotence, see the quotations in Suet. *Cal.* 22.1, 29.1, 30.1, 32.3, 33.

204 **His own sister.** I.e. Drusilla: see Suet. *Cal.* 24, who alleges incest with the other two sisters as well (so too Dio LIX 3.6, Vict. *Caes.* 3.10, Orosius VII 5.9 etc). Cf. Syme *AA* 186: 'dire hazards and humiliations reinforced ties of affection in the last surviving members of a doomed family.' But Barrett (85) is sceptical, pointing to the silence of Philo, Seneca and Tacitus on the subject.

The Romans' hatred. Because incest offends the gods (Catullus

64.403–4). See on 158 above: J.'s main source continues to believe in popular hostility to Gaius.

Unheard of for generations.   Since P. Clodius and his sisters (Plutarch *Cicero* 29.3–4, etc)? When asked by Gaius whether he too slept with his sister, Passienus Crispus diplomatically replied 'not yet' (scholiast on Juvenal IV 81).

205 **Not one.**   Unfair: Gaius did a great deal of building in his short reign (Barrett 192–212, cf. Balsdon 175–8), and not all of it was self-indulgent. His concern for the corn supply (the Rhegium harbour) and the water supply (Pliny *NH* XXXVI 122, Frontinus *De aquis* 13, Suet. *Cal.* 21 on his aqueducts) was overshadowed by Claudius, who completed the projects and took the credit; see Barrett 194f, Levick 109–11.

Rhegium and Sicily.   Suet. *Cal.* 24.2 and 51.1 (cf. 20.1, 22) for Gaius' visit to Sicily in the summer of 38.

207 **Useless expenditure.**   Examples in Suet. *Cal.* 37, Dio LIX 2; see in general Barrett 224–6.

208 **Orator.**   Suet. *Cal.* 53, Dio LIX 19.3–6; cf. *Suda* s.v. 'Gaios' (supposedly the author of a book on rhetorical theory); see Barrett 47f.

Natural facility.   Cf. Tac. *Ann.* XIII 3 on his forcefulness (*vis*), Suet. *Cal.* 53.1 for the effect of his anger.

Practice.   Suet. *Cal.* 53.2 (cf. 50.1 for facial expressions).

209 **Study.**   Cf. Syme *AA* 441: 'The Caesars of the first dynasty, although apart from Augustus they might be called monsters, were all men of high culture and uncommon intelligence, so a sober writer in late Antiquity avers' (Vict. *Caes.* 8.7); Syme's footnote adds 'Caligula is not excluded. Observe the remarkable tribute in Josephus.' See Barrett 48f on Gaius' literary-critical observations (Suet. *Cal.* 34.2). For emperors and culture in general, see Andrew Wallace-Hadrill, *Suetonius* (London 1983) 83–6; and on 164 above.

Tiberius.   For Tiberius' literary tastes, see Tac. *Ann.* IV 58.1, Suet. *Tiberius* 56, 70; for his cultural background in general, see A.F. Stewart, *Journal of Roman Studies* 67 (1977) 76–90.

An apt pupil.   Gaius was with Tiberius on Capri from 31 to 37 (aged 19 to 25). 'From the entourage of the old magician on the island, what lesson was Caligula to learn save craft, servility and the future licence of illimitable power?' (Syme *Tac.* 436). Given Tiberius' scholarly tastes, that judgement is a little one-sided.

210   **Effect of power.**   See on 201 above for Gaius' character before coming
       to power. Here, as Noè points out (105f), J.'s view that power corrupted
       him presupposes a two-stage interpretation of his reign. At *Ant.* XVIII
       256, J. reports two years of 'really magnanimous' rule; Philo (*Leg.* 67)
       calls him 'excellent, humane, fair and liberal'—all qualities associated
       with good education—until his illness in late 37; according to Plutarch
       (*Antony* 87.4, though some editors emend the text), 'he ruled with
       distinction for a short time'.
       Casually.   See 172 above for the caprice of tyrants.

211   **Friends.**   See on 89 above; also M. Lepidus (20 above), Macro (Suet.
       Cal. 26.1), Passienus Crispus (scholiast on Juvenal IV 81), L. Vitellius
       (Dio LIX 27.6).
       Their conspiracy.   Cf. 211 above (Clemens' speech). J.'s source was
       no doubt thinking of Vinicianus (96 above); possibly also Valerius
       Asiaticus (102 and 159 above).
       Cost him his life.   Timpe (*RG* 479) plausibly suggests that this ended a
       book in J.'s source, as Tac. *Ann.* VI ends with the death of Tiberius (and
       an obituary) and XII with the death of Claudius. But Timpe assumes
       also—and draws far-reaching conclusions from the assumption—that
       J. continued with the same source for the next part of his narrative.
       That, I think, is unlikely: see below.

212-28   The narrative of Claudius' discovery and adoption by the Praetorian
          Guard repeats at greater length two items J. has already dealt with
          (the doublets are 162/214 and 163f/225), admits a more hostile view
          of the Senate (224, 228), and assumes a popular enthusiasm for the
          Principate, and for Claudius in particular, which is inconsistent with
          the attitude expressed in the previous passage (228, contrast 189, 191,
          194, 204). The natural assumption in that J. has turned to a different
          source.

212   **I mentioned above.**   At 103.
       Squeezed into.   Text and meaning uncertain. With Niese's reading
       (*kateilemmenos*, passive), J. could mean that Claudius 'was cut off' (i.e.
       from the theatre) and sought a hiding-place in the palace complex;
       but Schreckenberg's one-letter emendation (p. 42 above) gives a better
       sense.
       Narrow alley.   See on 104 above. If Claudius saw the heads being

carried past (216 below), he was probably not indoors. According to Suetonius (*Claud.* 10.1, see on 101 above), Claudius was among the crowd kept away from the emperor by the assassins, and made his way to a room in the imperial complex called the 'Hermaeum'; when he heard about the murder he crept out to a nearby balcony (*solarium*) and hid behind the curtains that covered the door. Dio (LX 1.2) says merely that he hid in a dark corner. Momigliano (808–10) was clearly wrong to suppose that J., Dio and Suetonius all followed the same source; see on 99–113 above, and Noè 113.

Noble birth.   See on 164 above.

213   **Private citizen.**   See Suet. *Claud.* 3–6; Levick 2.1–5. Gaius made him consul for two months in 37 (Suet. *Claud.* 7, Levick 2.5f).

Devoted to scholarship.   See on 164 above, where J.'s source implausibly cites Claudius' scholarly nature as an argument for the Praetorians to make him emperor (contrast 217 and 223 below). The context here, evidently from a different source, is much more realistic: *pace* Jung and Levick (see on 64–9 above), Claudius did not expect to be taken seriously in politics.

Especially in Greek.   Claudius had written two major works in Greek: a *History of Carthage* in eight books and an *Etruscan History* in twenty (Suet. *Claud.* 42.2).

Distanced himself.   So far as he could: see on 13 above.

214   **The crowd.**   See on 101 above.

Undisciplined as mercenary bodyguards.   Text and meaning very uncertain. Elsewhere, J.'s word for bodyguards (*somatophylakes*) refers to the Praetorian Guard (221, 237?, 247, 267).

The Praetorians.   J.'s phrase (*hoi peri to strategikon kaloumenon*) no doubt translates *in praetorio* in his Latin source (cf. Pliny *NH* VII 82, XXV 17); see Hugh J. Mason, *Greek Terms for Roman Institutions* (Toronto 1974) 86.

Council of war.   Already reported, no doubt from a different source, at 161–5 above.

215   **Engaged on vengeance.**   See 119–22 above.

216   **Bewildered.**   Timpe (*RG* 481) compares the undignified portrayal of Claudius' terror (218 etc, Suet. *Claud.* 10.1) with Seneca's malicious satire in the *Apocolocyntosis*. Could J.'s source here be Seneca's friend Fabius Rusticus (Tac. *Ann.* XIII 20.2)?

Asprenas and the others.   See 123–6 and 142 above.

Accessible by a few steps.   I.e. Suetonius' 'balcony' (see on 212 above)? But the stories differ: according to Suetonius (*Claud.* 10.2), the soldier saw Claudius' feet below the curtain.

217   **Gratus.**   A private soldier (*miles gregarius*), who happened to be 'hurrying about' (Suet. *Claud.* 10.2); the soldiers were looting the palace, and no doubt Gratus thought Claudius was worth robbing (Dio LX 1.2–3). Aurelius Victor (*Caes.* 3.16) calls him 'Vimius, a centurion from Epirus', but that is in the context of reflections—topical for Victor as a fourth-century imperial bureaucrat—about the corruption of the Roman army by the employment of 'barbarians': see H.W. Bird, *Sextus Aurelius Victor, a Historiographical Study* (Liverpool 1984) 42.

A Germanicus.   When the elder Drusus died in 9 BC after conquering Germany for Augustus, the Senate decreed that his descendants should have the right to use the *cognomen* 'Germanicus' (Suet. *Claud.* 1.3). His elder son was Germanicus Caesar, Gaius' father; his younger son was Claudius, who began using the name when his brother was adopted into the Julian *gens* in AD 4 (Suet. *Claud.* 2.1). Gaius' full title as emperor was 'C. Caesar Augustus Germanicus', and he made the most of being Germanicus' son (Smallwood nos. 33, 82–5); for Germanicus' reputation, see on 223 below.

Let's carry him off.   Contrast 165 above, where the kidnap is planned in advance.

218   **Terrified.**   See on 216 above. Timpe (*UK* 84 n. 1) implies that Claudius was afraid of the republicans in the Senate; Levick (35) suggests that his fear may not have been genuine, and that Gratus may have been actively looking for him. Both interpretations are inconsistent with what J. says. Naturally, Claudius assumed that the Praetorians would do what they were paid for, and look for likely culprits.

He begged them.   According to Suetonius (*Claud.* 10.2), he fell at Gratus' feet.

219   **The gods.**   Cf. 167 above (Sentius' speech to the Senate).

What's best for the world.   A Stoic view: see for instance Seneca *De ira* II 27.1–2, *De beneficiis* VII 31.4. (See on 216 above: from Seneca's friend Fabius Rusticus?)

Throne of your ancestors.   A familiar phrase when used of foreign kings (e.g. Livy xxxix 53.4 on Demetrius, Lucan iv 690 on Juba); Tacitus (*Hist.* i 40) uses it to distinguish Parthian kings from Roman *imperatores,* but already under Augustus a constellation had been named 'Caesar's Throne' (Pliny *NH* ii 178). Claudius was not a Caesar (see on 164 above); but he was the brother of one (Germanicus, by adoption), and no doubt that was good enough for Gratus.

221 **There were some black looks.** Text uncertain. One would expect the black looks to come from the bystanders (222) *against* the Praetorians.

Kept out of politics. See on 213 above.

Shared the dangers. See on 13 above.

Referred to the consuls. Because the Senate was supposed to be investigating the murder (158)?

222 **The crowd.** See 101 and 204 above.

Litter-bearers. Those of Gaius were more courageous (see on 109 above).

Physical collapse. Because of his terror (220), or his disability (probably cerebral palsy, Levick 13–14)? If the latter, the desertion of the litter-bearers will have incapacitated him.

223 **They had reached.** J. uses the verb *antilambanesthai* in a Thucydidean sense: cf. Thuc. iii 22.8 (escape of the Plataeans), vii 77.6 (speech of Nicias).

The public area. J.'s word (*to demosion*) can mean 'public treasury', and he uses it in that sense at *Ant.* xvi 164; see Hugh J. Mason, *Greek Terms for Roman Institutions* (Toronto 1974) 35. But that is clearly not the meaning here (*pace* Feldman 319). The word means simply 'public', and presumably indicates that they were outside the imperial property.

Open square. I.e. the Area Palatina (Aulus Gellius *Noctes Atticae* xx 1.2).

As the story goes. Another comment for a non-Roman readership? See on 3 and 158 above. Ovid too (*Tristia* iii 1.31–40) takes it for granted that Rome was first founded precisely at this point on the Palatine, in front of Augustus' forecourt with the oak wreath and laurels. See Wiseman *Pal.* 251–4: no doubt the site of Romulus's original augury (the hut at 75 and 90 above?) was in the piazza immediately outside the imperial residence.

His brother Germanicus. See on 217 above: Suet. *Cal.* 1–7 for a mini-biography, Tac. *Ann.* II 73.2–3 for a 'laudation grotesque in its disproportion' (Syme *Tac.* 492). For Germanicus' enduring popularity, see Dio LVIII 8.2, LIX 3.8, Suet. *Claud.* 7, Smallwood nos. 83, 97, Tac. *Ann.* XI 12.1, XII 2.3, XIV 7.4.

224 **Calculation.** As at 162–5. Contrast the reaction of the Germans (120f above).

Grasping. Cf. 228 and 236 below on rapacity and arrogance; J.'s source for this passage (contrast 166–89) emphasises the shortcomings of the Senate.

The last time. I.e. the fifties BC (cf. 228 below).

225 **A republic was unworkable.** See on 163 above. Cf. Tac. *Hist.* I 84 (Otho's speech to the Praetorians) on the history of Rome 'a regibus usque ad principes', with 450 years of the Republic omitted.

Someone else's. The same point is made at 163 above.

Remembering his debt. See C.H.V. Sutherland, *Roman History and Coinage 44 BC–AD 69* (Oxford 1987) 74–7 on the Claudian coin-types that honoured the Praetorians (Smallwood no. 36).

Reward. See on 165 above.

226 **New contingents.** Groups who had been looting other parts of the imperial property? Or arriving from the barracks?

Wheeled round. Since Gratus and Claudius had emerged from the imperial residence, if the Guards were facing them during the discussion, they would have to turn left to go back down the street to the Velia, and from there to the barracks via the Oppian; they would naturally avoid the Forum area, which was controlled by the urban cohorts (Suet. *Claud.* 10.3, cf. Dio LIX 30.3).

Claudius' litter. See 222 above.

To the barracks. According to Suetonius (*Claud.* 10.2) Claudius was terrified and unhappy, and those of the populace who saw him being carried by 'pitied him as an innocent man being taken to execution' (see on 218 above).

227 **A clear difference.** See on 158 above; inconsistent with 189 and 191, which must come from a different source.

Slavery. See on 181 above.

Insolence. I.e. *hybris*: see on 1 above.

228 **Rapacity.** So also at 224 above; Charlesworth (117) compares Tac. *Ann.* I 2.2 on the avarice of republican magistrates. Senatorial abuse of

power was the reason for the institution of the tribunate of the *plebs*: see for instance Cicero *Pro Cornelio* quoted in Asconius 76C (*nimia dominatio*), Sallust *Histories* I fr. 11M (*iniuriae, saevitia*).

Protection for themselves. For this aspect of the Principate, symbolised by the *tribunicia potestas* (Tac. *Ann.* I 2.1), see Z. Yavetz, *Plebs and Princeps* (Oxford 1969), esp. chapters 5 and 6.

Delighted. So too Suet. *Claud.* 10.4; contrast 189 above.

The days of Pompey. I.e. the fifties BC (cf. 224 above).

229–36   The Senate's embassy to Claudius. The decision to send the embassy must have been taken at the meeting of the Senate described by J.'s main source at 158–89; see on 160 above for items omitted there. According to Suetonius (*Claud.* 10.3), Claudius was summoned to the Senate 'for consultation', and replied that he was being forcibly detained. J.'s narrative here differs substantially from his earlier account at *Bell.* II 205–10; see on 236 below.

229   **A deputation.** The only named members are the two tribunes (234 below); cf. Suet. *Claud.* 10.3 (tribunes), Dio LX 1.4 (tribunes 'and others'). The inclusion of the tribunes implied that the message came from the Senate and *People* of Rome. But also, 'the senior magistrates were probably fully engaged and not to be risked as potential hostages, and tribunes' persons were sacrosanct' (Levick 31). According to J.'s later narrative (244–5 below), which is inconsistent with what he wrote at *Bell.* II 205, King Agrippa was also one of the ambassadors.

230   **Rule of law.** See on 15 above. Cf. Dio LX 1.4: 'submit to the Senate and People of Rome, and to the laws.'

The danger you were in. See on 13 and 221 above.

Hated the burden of tyranny. Claudius' father (Tac. *Ann.* I 33.2, Suet. *Tiberius* 50.1, *Claud.* 1.4) and brother (Tac. *Ann.* II 82.2) were both supposed to have favoured a return to republican government.

Drunken bully. Claudius was notoriously fond of wine: Suet. *Claud.* 5.1, 33.1, 40.1, Dio LXI 34.2.

231   **Blamelessly unpolitical.** See 213, 221 above.

Votes of a free people. Cf. 184 above.

Praise for excellence. Literally 'virtue': see on 171 and 172 above.

232   **But if.** After the invitation to co-operate (which no doubt included the summons to the Senate reported in Suet. *Claud.* 10.3) came the

threat of force (which at *Bell.* II 205 is called the Senate's declaration of war).

A large part. The urban cohorts: see on 188 above.

Stores of weapons. Where? At a similar crisis in 121 BC, M. Fulvius Flaccus armed his supporters with the captured spoils of his Gallic triumph, which were presumably hung up in the vestibule of his house (Plutarch *Gaius Gracchus* 15.1, cf. Suet. *Nero* 38.2 for houses adorned with *spolia*). But perhaps the reference is to gladiators' weapons (see on 253 below); for gladiators as bodyguards in the late Republic, see A.W. Lintott, *Violence in Republican Rome* (Oxford 1968) 83–5.

Slaves. This was a bluff: even without Agrippa's advice, they knew armed slaves were no match for the Praetorians. See on 242–3 below.

233   **Hope and chance.** In the most pointed of all his Thucydidean reminiscences, J. gives to the Senate's spokesmen the same arguments used in 415 BC by the doomed Melians against the ruthless power of Athens: Thucydides V 102 (hope and chance), 104 (the gods help the righteous).

234   **Veranius.** Q. Veranius, later consul (in 49) and imperial legate in Britain (in 57–8): see A.R. Birley, *The Roman Government of Britain* (Oxford 2005) 37–43.

Brocchus. Probably the Sertorius Brocchus known from coins as governor of an eastern province under Claudius (*Prosopographia Imperii Romani* S 394).

Tribunes. See on 229 above.

Fell at Claudius' feet. For this extreme of body language, evidently not incompatible with senatorial dignity, cf. (e.g.) Cicero *Ad Atticum* I 14.5, IV 2.4, X 4.3, Suet. *Julius* 20.4.

235   **Let him accept it.** Clearly an improvised compromise proposal, envisaging the sort of non-tyrannical principate Claudius himself offers at 246; Timpe (*RG* 488f) is surely wrong to imply that it was part of the Senate's message.

236   **Arrogance.** See on 224 above.

Caution. Suetonius (*Claud.* 10.3) emphasises Claudius' fear.

Confidence of the soldiers. They outnumbered the urban cohorts by three to one, and they had the fortified barracks as their base (cf. Suet. *Claud.* 10.3, 'within the *vallum*').

King Agrippa. The grandson of Herod 'the Great' of Judaea (Barrett

34–7), and an important figure in J.'s work; indeed, the whole narrative of Gaius' death and Claudius' accession is a digression in the story of Agrippa's adventures (see *Ant.* XVIII 142–255, 289–301, XIX 274–7, 292–359).

See Schwartz 1–38 for J.'s various sources on Agrippa, one of which was evidently a novelistic biography of the king with no good claim to historical accuracy (Schwartz 33–7, calling it *VAgr*). As a result, what Agrippa did for Claudius is narrated quite differently by J. in his two historical works: at *Bell.* II 206–10 Agrippa is little more than a go-between, but the version of events here, inserted by J. into his Roman narrative, clearly comes from *VAgr* (Schwartz 29), and may well be fictional. Dio (LX 8.2) also reports Agrippa's help in putting Claudius in power, but gives no details.

237–45   An interpolated 'flash-back' to explain how Agrippa came to be in the position to advise Claudius to take a tough line. As Timpe points out (*RG* 502, *UK* 89 n. 3), the insertion is awkward and confusing; but I think he is wrong to infer that there were *two* embassies from the Senate to Claudius.

237   **Held in honour.**   See *Ant.* XVIII 289–300.

    Attended to the corpse.   Presumably after the murder of Caesonia and the little girl (see on 195 above). Later the body of Gaius was taken to the Lamian Gardens on the Esquiline for a hasty part-cremation and burial (Suet. *Cal.* 56); but clearly not by Agrippa (*pace* Barrett 167, 174).

    Gaius was alive.   Was this the origin of the 'rival story' that circulated in the theatre (134 above)? The reference to doctors suggests it; but by the time Agrippa got to Gaius' body, the theatre crowd had surely dispersed.

238   **When he heard.**   Contrast *Bell.* II 206, where Agrippa is summoned simultaneously by Claudius (at the barracks) and by the Senate, and chooses Claudius.

    Ready to give way.   As in 42 to Arruntius Scribonianus (Suet. *Claud.* 35.2), and in 48 to C. Silius (Tac. *Ann.* XI 31).

    Urged him on.   At *Bell.* II 206, Agrippa realises that Claudius already has the power to make himself Caesar.

239   **Returned home.**   Contrast *Bell.* II 207–8, where he is sent by Claudius

to the Senate with the message reported at 246 below. The detail about Agrippa's subterfuge suggests a novelistic source (see on 236 above).

Summoned to the Senate.   See on 238 above.

After a party.   I.e., it was now late evening or night. Had Chaerea already been given the password? See 186 above, the only other indication of time (but from a different source).

240   **The honour of the Senate.**   Mere flattery: for the reality of 'kings at the centre of power', see D.C. Braund, *Rome and the Friendly King* (London 1984) 55–73. Agrippa was regarded as one of Gaius' instructors in tyranny (Dio LIX 24.1).

241   **Laid claim to.**   J. uses a Thucydidean expression (Thuc. I 140.1, II 51.5).

242   **An abundance of weapons.**   See on 232 above.

Giving slaves their freedom.   Cf. 232 above. Arming freed slaves was contemplated only in times of dire emergency, as in AD 6 and 9, after the revolts of Pannonia and Germany (Suet. *Augustus* 25.2, Velleius II 111.1). J.'s source may have had in mind the moment in 69 when the Praetorians thought the senators were arming their slaves to murder Otho (Tac. *Hist.* I 80).

243   **Trained in warfare.**   Their most recent experience was with Gaius in Gaul and Germany: details in Barrett 125–39.

244   **My advice.**   The Senate hardly needed to be told this; but J.'s source at this point was concerned to maximise Agrippa's importance.

An embassy.   I.e. the one reported at 229 above (*pace* Timpe *UK* 90).

245   **He briefed Claudius.**   The 'flash-back' has now caught up with the narrative at 236 above (Agrippa's advice).

246–53   Claudius' reply and the Senate's reaction. At *Bell.* II 207–10, Agrippa delivers the reply and is sent back with a defiant message from the Senate. He then delivers a further reply from Claudius: if there must be a civil war, let it be outside the city. As Timpe observes (*RG* 502), that account of Agrippa as a 'neutral' go-between is perfectly credible, and the negotiations recorded in *Bell.* may well be genuine. In *Ant.*, however, J. uses a Roman source which ignores Agrippa, interpolated with an account which exaggerates his importance at an earlier stage in the events.

246   **Monarchy in name.**   Cf. Dio LIX 6.1 (Gaius), Tac. *Ann.* XII 4 (Nero): 'such a speech as was made once by nearly every other emperor during

the century' (Balsdon 27). Timpe however (*RG* 488–9) sees it as a genuine offer of joint government, an opportunity (thrown away by the Senate die-hards) to obtain a principate by consent.

Vicissitudes.   See on 13 above.

247   **The assembled troops.**   A formal parade of the Praetorians in arms (Suet. *Claud.* 10.4); according to Suetonius, it took place the following day, after a popular demonstration in Claudius' favour at the Senate meeting described below. For the numismatic evidence for Claudius' dependence on the Praetorians, see on 225 above.

Five thousand denarii.   I.e. 20,000 sesterces. Suetonius (*Claud.* 10.4), who gives the figure as 15,000, comments that Claudius was the first of the Caesars to buy the loyalty of his troops. Barrett (175f) demurs, unnecessarily: it was fifteen or twenty times what Gaius had given them to celebrate his accession (Dio LIX 2.1). As Levick comments (32f), this 'enormous sum [was] intended to shake the loyalty of the urban cohorts to the Senate'—and it evidently did so.

248   **While it was still night.**   No doubt after Agrippa's further report from Claudius had made it clear that civil war was inevitable (J. *Bell.* II 209f).

The temple of Jupiter.   See on 158 above. This is the temple of Jupiter Victor on the Capitol, attested on a fragmentary calendar recently recovered from the Via Ardeatina: see Filippo Coarelli, *Palatium* (Rome 2012) 241–6. The Capitol was defensible, and the consuls had already transferred the treasury there (Dio LIX 30.3).

Despaired of the liberty.   See on 180 and 181 above. Timpe (*RG* 495) contrasts the vigour of Chaerea.

249   **A hundred senators.**   'The most strong-minded of a putative 600' (Levick 31). Most of the crowded Senate of the day before (161 above) will have dispersed at the time Chaerea took the password (186 above).

Shout from the soldiers.   One individual soldier, according to J. *Bell.* II 211; the crowd gathered outside, according to Suet. *Claud.* 10.4; both versions specify support for Claudius rather than, as here, a rival candidate from the Senate.

250   **One man.**   See on 163 and 225 above; if a strong candidate emerged and defeated Claudius, the urban cohorts would profit from his victory.

Lost the liberty.   I.e. the issue was now merely who the next emperor would be. In J.'s earlier version (*Bell.* II 205), the election of a suitable emperor from the Senate was a possibility from the start; Suetonius, however (*Cal.* 60), is clear that the conspirators did not want a successor.

251 **There were some.**   Including Vinicianus himself (J.'s 'Minucianus'), according to Dio LX 15.1. Both the men named by J. here were honoured by Claudius with second consulships (in 45 and 46), and soon afterwards destroyed by Messallina (Vinicius, Dio LX 27.4; Asiaticus, Tac. *Ann.* XI 1–2); and Vinicianus committed suicide after the failure of Arruntius Scribonianus' rising in 42 (Dio LX 15.5). Perhaps J.'s source, like Tacitus later, was conscious of the *capax imperii* theme, the fate of potential emperors: see Syme *Tac.* 58 (citing J. *Bell.* II 205 in n. 4), 380f, 485f.

Illustrious birth.   'Senators of birth and rank still counted ... The assassination of Caligula brought noble pedigrees into debate and notoriety' (Syme *Tac.* 381 and 385, on *capaces imperii*).

Marcus Vinicius.   See on 102 above. For the text here, see Swan 149–55.

Julia.   I.e. Julia Livilla (Tac. *Ann.* VI 15.1), now about 23 or 24; she had been disgraced and banished in connection with the Lepidus affair in 39 (see on 20 above). After Gaius' death, she returned and with her sister Agrippina saw to his proper cremation (Suet. *Cal.* 59), but was then sent into exile again and put to death by the jealous Messallina (Dio LX 8.5, 'adultery with Seneca').

252 **Valerius Asiaticus.**   See on 102 and 159 above; Levick 61–3 for his fall.

Minucianus.   I.e. Annius Vinicianus: see on 18 above. Barrett (108, cf. 33) suggests he was the son of M. Vinicius' sister.

A massacre.   As foreseen by the tribunes (234 above) and by Claudius in his second message (J. *Bell.* II 209f). So too if Galba had brought his army from Germany, or Arruntius Scribonianus his from Dalmatia, as they were both invited to do (Suet. *Galba* 7.1, Dio LX 15.2).

253 **Gladiators.**   See on 232 above. Two praetors each year were responsible for giving public gladiatorial shows (Dio LIX 14.2); Claudius put a stop to it (Dio LX 5.6), no doubt as a result of his anxieties at this time.

Night watch.   Seven cohorts of freedmen who acted as Rome's fire-brigade: see Lawrence Keppie, *The Making of the Roman Army* (London 1984) 189; J.S. Rainbird, *Papers of the British School at Rome* 54 (1986) 147–69.

Rowers from the fleet.   See Keppie pp. 186–7. The west-coast fleet was based at Misenum on the Bay of Naples, but there was a detachment at Ostia which could quickly get to Rome (Suet. *Vespasian* 8.3). Nero in his last days raised a 'fleet legion' (*legio classica*) from the Misenum sailors, and J.'s source at this point may well have had in mind Galba's massacre of the *legio classica* at the Milvian bridge in the autumn of 68: see Tac. *Hist.* I 6, with G.E.F. Chilver's commentary (Oxford 1979, pp. 52–4).

Some … others. How many were there? J.'s source may have named more than the two mentioned at 251–2.

254–63 The desertion of the urban cohorts. The focus of the narrative now returns to Chaerea (not mentioned since 200).

254 **At daybreak.** On 23 January: see on 85 above.

Addressing the soldiers. If the news of Claudius' donative to the Praetorians (247 above) had reached the urban cohorts, Chaerea and his colleagues would know they had a problem of morale to contend with.

Their new leader. Claudius? Or someone chosen by the Senate (250)?

255 **The Senate was paralysed.** The contrast with the resolute Senate of the previous day must have been obvious enough at the time; but it may also be partly due to J.'s change of source (see on 224 above). No mention is made here of the consuls; the Senate is portrayed as a mere leaderless mass.

Gaius' assassins. Contrast 182–4 and 188–9 above, where the Senate and the assassins are as one. But there is a hint of discord at 161, which may reflect different priorities from the start (see on 250 above).

Give in to the soldiers. Cf. Tac. *Hist.* I 18 (Galba's old-fashioned insistence on discipline): 'we aren't equal to that now.'

257 **The Green faction.** For the four colours, of which the Blues and the Greens were most important, see Alan Cameron, *Circus Factions* (Oxford 1976) ch. 3.

A fan of his. For Eutychus, and Gaius' chariot-racing enthusiasms in general, see Suet. *Cal.* 55.2f, Dio LIX 14.5–7; Barrett 45f.

Eutychus' horses. Including the great Incitatus, whom Gaius planned to make a consul (Suet. *Cal.* 55.3), 'and would have done if he had lived' (Dio LIX 14.7).

258 **The head of Claudius.** This probably cost Chaerea his life, since he was executed for plotting to kill not only Gaius but Claudius as well (Dio LX 3.4, Suet. *Claud.* 11.1).

A madman.   See on 1 above.

An idiot.   See on 216 above.

259   **Oath of loyalty.**   247 above.

Left defenceless.   As Agrippa had warned (241 above).

260   **Anger.**   A known characteristic of Claudius (Suet. *Claud.* 38.1–2).

Abused each other.   As in Sallust *Catiline* 53.1 (after Cato's speech).

261   **Sabinus.**   See on 46 above.

To kill himself.   And he did so, later (273 below).

A government of slaves.   *Doulokratia* (see on 14 above): Suet. *Claud.*
25.5, 28, 29.1.

262   **Test Claudius' intentions.**   Probably Chaerea still hoped that the
timid Claudius (Suet. *Claud.* 35–6) would not stand his ground; see on
238 above.

263–8   The Senate capitulates. The transition is very abrupt; one would expect
a reference to an official deputation, as perhaps implied at *Bell.* II 212.
A lacuna in the text? Or J. over-abbreviating his source?

263   **Quintus Pomponius.**   See on 160 above. As Timpe points out (*UK* 91),
no doubt both consuls went to the barracks, but only Pomponius is
mentioned because of the attack on him. At *Bell.* II 213 it is 'the leaders'
who are attacked.

Freedom.   As in his colleague's speech (167 etc).

Had not prevented it.   At *Bell.* II 213, Agrippa has to warn Claudius
of the danger.

264   **Aponius.**   Perhaps Aponius Saturninus, who fell asleep at one of
Gaius' auctions and awoke to find he had bought thirteen gladiators
(Suet. *Cal.* 38.4); his fictional career is in Hubert Monteilhet, *Neropolis*
(Paris 1984, Eng. trans. 1988).

265   **King Agrippa.**   See on 236 above. At *Bell.* II 213 he intervenes at a
slightly earlier stage (see on 263 above), but says much the same: if
Claudius didn't restrain the Praetorians, 'he would lose the very people
who could make his reign glorious, and find himself the ruler of a
desert' (trans. G.A. Williamson).

266   **Summoned the Senate.**   At *Bell.* II 214, J. makes it clear that Claudius,
having warmly greeted the senators, *immediately* left the barracks
with them 'to present to God thank-offerings for his accession'. No
doubt the thanksgiving—to the *gods*, of course—was equally for the

averting of civil war (see on 252 above). It may have been at this point that the Senate 'voted him all the powers of the Principate' (Dio LX 1.4)—including the right to use the names 'Caesar' and 'Augustus' (Levick 42).

On the Palatine. See Talbert 117f for Senate meetings on the Palatine. They were held in the library and portico of the Apollo temple—that is, within the imperial complex itself (Ovid *Fasti* IV 951-4). Claudius was reclaiming the emperor's space.

Much brutality. Until Claudius was more sure of his position, security was very strict (Dio LX 3.2f, Suet. *Claud.* 35); the Praetorians were determined to protect 'their' emperor.

267 **Pollio.** I.e. Rufrius Pollio (Dio LX 23.2). His colleague Catonius Justus (Dio LX 18.4) was probably appointed at the same time; the prefects who had failed to protect Gaius (see on 37 above) could hardly expect to keep their jobs.

268 **Advisers.** I.e. his *consilium*, which at this time probably consisted of his new prefects, Agrippa, and perhaps his freedmen. Forty friends and advisers of Claudius are named in the prosopographical index of J. Crook, *Consilium Principis* (Cambridge 1955), but few of them are likely to have been at his side so early.

A glorious one. See on 182 above. Claudius did not try to avenge Gaius, but declared an amnesty for the events of these two days (Suet. *Claud.* 11.1, Dio LX 3.5; Timpe *UK* 91).

Disloyalty. Timpe (*RG* 495-6) rightly draws attention to the cruel irony of J.'s source: in fact, Chaerea's loyalty was absolute, but it was to an old-fashioned ideal of Roman virtue inconsistent with the rule of emperors.

As a deterrent. Suetonius (*Claud.* 11.1) and Dio (LX 3.4) mention also Chaerea's declared intention to kill Claudius (see on 258 above); and Timpe suggests (*UK* 91) that another reason may have been the murder of Caesonia and the little girl (hence the emphasis on Lupus and Chaerea below, and the acquittal of Cornelius Sabinus). But J.'s source mentions only the least sympathetic motive.

269-73 Chaerea is executed. It seems that for this final scene J. returns briefly to his main source, for whom Chaerea was *sans peur et sans reproche*.

269 **Lupus.** See on 191 above.

Many other Romans. See on 167 above for the evocative use of the word 'Roman'. How many others were executed? Dio (LX 3.4) just says 'certain others'; according to Suetonius, who thought Caesonia was killed by a centurion, it was 'a few tribunes and centurions' (Suet. *Claud.* 11.1, cf. *Cal.* 59).

It is said. A sign of a change of source?

270   **A wolf.** J. does not translate the Latin pun on Lupus' name; see on 130, 202 and 214 above for similar traces of his Latin source.

The place of execution. Outside the Esquiline Gate (Tac. *Ann.* II 2.3, XV 60.1, cf. Plautus *Miles Gloriosus* 359–60).

Chaerea asked. The tribune Subrius Flavus showed the same *sang-froid* in a similar situation in AD 65 (Tac. *Ann.* XV 67.4).

Held a sword. The soldier's reply is lost, and Niese accordingly marks a lacuna in the text. Robert Graves (*Claudius the God,* Penguin ed. 81) gives him a good line: 'I was a butcher in civil life.'

'Go,' he said. This is likely to be an embroidery by J.'s source (see on 105 and 106 above for similar effects). Presumably Chaerea, like Lupus, had been disarmed at the Palatine, so his sword would not be conveniently available. But since the earlier tyrannicide Cassius used on himself the dagger with which he had killed Caesar (Plutarch *Caesar* 69.3), no doubt the parallel was too good to miss.

271   **Made a bad exit.** See on 199 above, for the last scene in which Lupus had a role.

272   **A few days later.** 'A period for appeasing the dead (*placandis Manibus*) started at the sixth hour of 13 February and lasted either to the 21st (Feralia) or 22nd (Caristia or Cara Cognatio)': H.H. Scullard, *Festivals and Ceremonies of the Roman Republic* (London 1981) 74, on the Parentalia, when 'the living respectfully and lovingly carried out their duties to the friendly dead and thus secured their mutual well-being.'

Ingratitude. *Acharistia*, a bilingual pun on Caristia, the name of the festival on 22 February when families settled their quarrels (Ovid *Fasti* II 631f).

273   **So Chaerea ended.** See on 114 above.

Exonerated. Because he had not threatened Claudius' life or been involved in the killing of Gaius' wife and child? See on 268 above (Timpe *UK* 91).

Killed himself. As he had promised (261 above), and out of loyalty to Chaerea (Dio LX 3.5).

J. now returns to his Jewish theme, and in particular to the career of Agrippa (see on 236 above). But the Roman story had a sequel—the attempt by Vinicianus and Q. Pomponius (see on 160 and 251 above) to oust Claudius with the help of the legions of Arruntius Scribonianus, imperial legate of Dalmatia. It failed, and those involved were executed in a brutal reign of terror (Dio LX 15–16, Pliny *Letters* III 16).

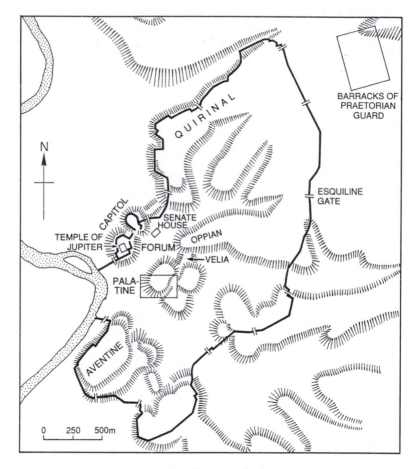

Figure 1 The site of Rome.
The rectangle at the Palatine represents the area mapped in fig. 2.

The Augustan Palatine

In the late Republic, the Palatine was largely occupied by the town houses of the Roman aristocracy. Already in the 30s BC, the young Caesar (who would later be Augustus) lived in one such house at a characteristically significant location, close to the site of the founder's 'august augury' that gave him his new name.[1]

He and his agents systematically bought up neighbouring houses; some of them he demolished in order to build the great temple of Apollo which was dedicated in 28 BC,[2] the others became part of a complex property consisting of various houses, but with a single formal entrance which by decree of the Senate in 27 BC was decorated with honorific laurels and the 'civic crown' above the door.[3]

Gaius, we are told,[4] extended the property to the northern corner of the Palatine, and gave it a direct access to the Forum. But he did not rebuild it as a unified palace; Josephus makes clear (117) that it was still a group of individual houses, with alleys and streets between them like the one where Gaius met his death (104, 116) and the one where Claudius hid from the guards (212).

It was all destroyed in the great fire of AD 64.[5] Only a few basement areas survived, some of them incorporated into the foundations of the great new purpose-built palaces with which Nero's architects exploited the huge area that had suddenly become available to them.[6] Two of the main blocks of the Neronian master-plan are easily detectable in the modern Palatine site: first, a huge rectangular palace on the summit of the hill, excavated in the 1920s and 1930s (the remains are mainly Domitianic, but the ground plan is likely to be Neronian), which was known as the *domus Augustana* or *Augustiana*;[7] and second, a large rectangular platform artificially projecting out over the north-west side of the hill on enormous substructions (now the site of the Farnese Gardens), which supported a house and gardens known as the *domus Tiberiana*.[8]

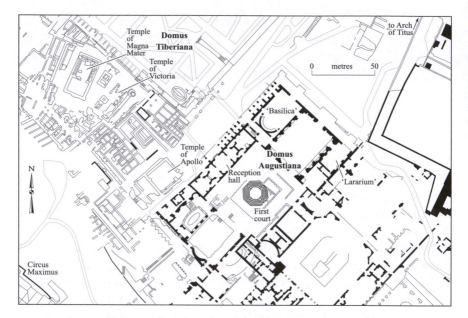

Figure 2a The central and western Palatine, showing the post-Neronian palaces.

Why were the palaces given these names? The only plausible answer is that they respectively incorporated the original sites—much smaller, of course—of the houses of Augustus and Tiberius.

That inevitable conclusion was resisted for a long time, because in the 1950s Gianfilippo Carettoni, excavating the remains of a late-republican house on the slope immediately north-west of the Apollo temple, came to the conclusion that it was built as an integral part of the temple project, and must therefore have been the house of Augustus himself.[9] More recent investigation has cast doubt on that, suggesting that most of the house was in fact destroyed in the course of the creation of the temple;[10] this new information fits precisely with what the historians say about the future Augustus in the 30s BC, buying up neighbouring properties in order to build on their sites.[11]

So we may return to the natural meaning of *domus August(i)ana*, and confidently place the original house of Augustus—the nucleus of the 'imperial residence' that consisted of houses with streets and alleys between them (103–4, 116–17)—in the area covered by the great palace on the summit

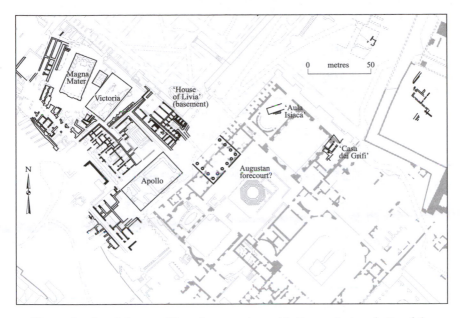

Figure 2b Surviving pre-Neronian remains, with the conjectured site of the Augustan *vestibulum*. It is not known when the main part of the 'House of Livia' was demolished; 36 BC is a possibility.

of the hill. Surviving remains in the foundations of the palace—the 'Aula Isiaca' and the 'House of the Griffins', respectively below the rooms conventionally labelled 'Basilica' and 'Lararium' (fig. 2a)—presumably belonged to two of the neighbouring houses.

Although Augustus' house was not a grand one,[12] in front of its door it had a very substantial forecourt (*vestibulum*), large enough to accommodate a shrine of Vesta[13] and grand enough for the lying in state of the dead Augustus in AD 14.[14] It was probably the site of the altar to the *Numen* of Augustus, and therefore also of the Palatine Games.[15] We may reasonably imagine that the wooden benches of the temporary theatre were set up in the forecourt, looking out to a stage building at the historic hut (75, 90) in the piazza beyond.

At this point a further piece of evidence comes into play. The 'Sorrento base' is the remains of a rectangular altar or statue-base;[16] it was probably designed for the cult of Divus Augustus, since the reliefs on the sides all allude to the topography of the Augustan Palatine. The short side B, which

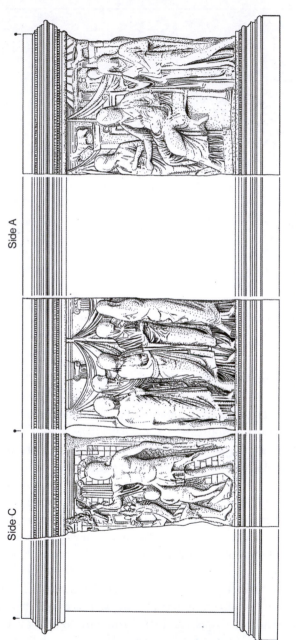

Side A

Side C

Figure 3   The 'Sorrento base', sides A and C.

survives complete, shows Apollo with Artemis, Leto and the Sibyl, and the Magna Mater appears on the surviving part of the long side D (one might guess at Romulus and Victory for the missing part of that scene).

The long side A and the short side C are shown in Figure 3: that they belong together topographically is clear from the continuous background of an Ionic colonnade. The missing central part of side A probably showed Augustus in the act of sacrificing to Vesta. The Vestal Virgins are at the left, and the goddess herself, flanked by two other divinities, is enthroned to the right in front of her round temple, within which the Palladion is just visible.[17] Side C, of which half is missing, was centred on the entrance to Augustus' house, with winged *amoretti* holding the 'civic crown' above it; in front sat the Genius of Augustus holding a cornucopia. To the right, Cupid leads Mars, or possibly Aeneas, towards (presumably) Venus, the ancestress of Augustus, who must have occupied the left-hand space.

What this double scene seems to show is Augustus' formal entrance and the Vesta temple both enclosed in a single Ionic portico. It is a reasonable surmise that the portico enclosed the forecourt, and was the one Josephus refers to (90) at the site of the temporary theatre. The altar (87) would be that of the *Numen Augusti*, iconographically represented as the seated Genius.[18]

But where exactly was this cityscape of forecourt and altar? If the forecourt did indeed contain the temporary theatre, and if the stage building of the theatre was indeed put up at the hut from where Romulus originally made his 'august augury' at the founding of the city, then a triangulation of three separate references in our literary sources may give us an answer. The first is in the history of Dionysius of Halicarnassus, who describes Romulus as making the augury from a 'clear space' with a view to the east, obviously on the summit of the hill.[19] The second is Ovid's casual comment that Rome 'was first founded' at a place on the Palatine next to Augustus' forecourt.[20] And the third is Josephus' own statement (223) that 'the open square on the Palatine' was where 'Rome was first settled'.

The main forecourt of the later palace was evidently on the north-east side, reached from a broad new avenue that ascended from the Velia (near the Arch of Titus).[21] At that point the ground is already sloping downwards, and the new palatial forecourt featured a grand staircase.[22] But steps are never mentioned in connection with the Augustan forecourt; there is no sign of a staircase on the 'Sorrento base'; and in any case the piazza at that point is too low to be a credible site for Romulus' *auguratorium*.

There was, however, another entrance to the palace on the north-west side, leading into an octagonal 'reception hall' (fig. 2a), and that fulfils the necessary conditions exactly.

At fig. 2b I offer a conjectural layout based on the assumption that the Augustan forecourt, and therefore also the site of the temporary theatre for the Palatine Games, roughly corresponded to the position of the reception hall and the suites on either side of it. I assume that the piazza in front of the forecourt was more extensive before the creation of the *domus Tiberiana* platform turned it into just a wide avenue running between the two palaces to the Apollo temple.[23] Of course there can be no certainty, but this reconstruction does at least account for what our sources say.

When Gaius eventually left his seat in the theatre, he and his party must have walked round through the portico to the formal entrance of the residence, which we may assume was in the centre of the forecourt. Once inside, Claudius, Vinicius, Asiaticus and the rest took the 'direct route' (103) to wherever lunch was being served, while Gaius turned off down the 'empty alleyway' (104) which would bring him to where the choirboys were rehearsing. Presumably the main party were heading south-east to somewhere roughly corresponding to the first great court of the later palace (fig. 2a). Unfortunately, we are not told whether Gaius turned off to the left or to the right.

According to Suetonius, the boys were rehearsing in a basement area (*crypta*), perhaps a room like the 'Aula Isiaca' below the so-called 'Basilica' at the northern corner of the palace (fig. 4). Indeed, if we combine the evidence of Josephus and Suetonius, and assume that Gaius turned off to the left, we might even imagine stairs leading down from the 'empty alleyway' to this very chamber. So it is just possible, though perhaps too good to be true, that pure chance has preserved the exact place where Gaius met his end. Wherever it was, the house where he was killed was haunted for years, until the fire destroyed it.[24]

Notes

1   Suet. *Augustus* 7.2, quoting Ennius' line 'After famous Rome was founded *augusto augurio*'; see on 75 and 223 above for the hut that served as Romulus' *auguratorium* (Wiseman *Pal.* 251–4).

2   Velleius II 81.3, Dio XLIX 15.5; cf. Suet. *Augustus* 29.3.

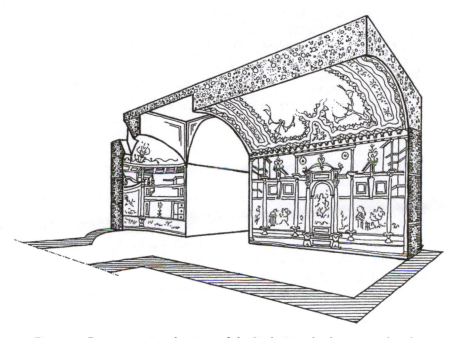

Figure 4 Reconstruction drawing of the 'Aula Isiaca', a basement chamber (*crypta*) about 7 metres high.

3 Augustus *Res gestae* 34.2, Dio LIII 16.4.
4 Suet. *Cal.* 22.2, cf. Dio LIX 28.5.
5 Tac. *Ann.* XV 39.1 ('the Palatine, the house and everything around was consumed'); Dio LXII 18.2 ('the whole of the Palatine hill was burned').
6 Details in Wiseman *Pal.* 262–4; recent suggestions that the developed *domus Augustana* and *domus Tiberiana* complexes date back to the early principate are inconsistent with the clear evidence that Augustus and Tiberius did not go in for lavish private building (Suet. *Augustus* 72, Tac. *Ann.* V 45.1); Gaius had the taste for it (207) but not the opportunity provided by the fire.
7 Confirmed by a recent inscription: *Année épigraphique* 2007 no. 252.
8 The identification is securely inferred from Tac. *Hist.* I 27 and Plutarch *Galba* 24.4.
9 Gianfilippo Carettoni, *Das Haus des Augustus auf dem Palatin* (Mainz 1983) 7–16.
10 Irene Iacopi and Giovanna Tedone, *Römische Mitteilungen* 112 (2006) 351–78; see Wiseman *Pal.* 255–7 for the consequences of their results.

11   Velleius Paterculus II 81.3, Dio XLIX 15.5.

12   Suet. *Augustus* 72.1 (*aedibus modicis*).

13   Ovid *Fasti* IV 950 (*limine*); note the derivation of *vestibulum* from Vesta at
      Fasti VI 303.

14   Suet. *Augustus* 100.2.

15   See note on 75 above.

16   See Tonio Hölscher in *Kaiser Augustus und die verlorene Republik*
      (Antikenmuseum Berlin 1988) 375–8.

17   Philip Hill, *The Monuments of Ancient Rome as Coin Types* (London 1989)
      32; *Corp. inscr. Lat.* X 6441 (a 'supervisor of the Palatine Palladion'). For the
      Palladion in the old Vesta temple, see Ovid *Fasti* VI 420–36, *Tristia* III 1.29,
      Dionysius II 66.5.

18   See D. Fishwick, 'Genius and Numen', *Harvard Theological Review* 62 (1969)
      356–67.

19   Dionysius II 5.1–2—probably from Varro, who is cited at II 21.2 and 47.4.

20   Ovid *Tristia* III 1.32, with the forecourt described at 33–48.

21   Filippo Coarelli, *Palatium: Il Palatino dalle origini all'impero* (Rome 2012)
      486–91; Wiseman *Pal.* 261–2.

22   For the 'steps of the *Palatium*' see Tac. *Hist.* I 29, III 74, Suet. *Nero* 8 (anachro-
      nistic?), *Vitellius* 15.2, Dio LXXVIII 55.5.

23   Most plans of the Palatine show the so-called 'house of Livia' projecting into
      this avenue, but that is an illusion: the basement apartments of the house,
      which are all that survive, were below the level of the pavement. Since the
      house evidently dates from the first half of the first century BC, it is possible
      that they were below the level of the Augustan piazza too, and that the main
      part of the house was destroyed after only a few decades.

24   Suet. *Cal.* 58.4 (*crypta*), 59 (haunted).

APPENDIX 2

Cluvius Rufus

The Cluvii came from Campania, the most hellenised area of Italy, and by the first century BC were well known in commerce and finance in the Greek cities of Asia Minor.[1] They were also of long-standing senatorial rank. Cluvii had been praetors in 178(?), 173 and 172 BC; two generations later a Cluvius, praetor or proconsul, was honoured by the business-men of Delos in or about 103 BC; two generations later again, a Cluvius who had been elected consul but prevented from holding office was granted consular rank by the young Caesar in 29 BC.[2]

Cluvius Rufus the historian was therefore a *nobilis,* and if Josephus is right to call him an ex-consul in January 41, he could have been born as late as AD 8.[3] That would put him in his late fifties when he acted as the announcer for Nero's public stage performances at the *Neronia* of AD 65 (and again on the emperor's tour of Greece in 66–67). Since Nero had the two Praetorian Prefects to carry his lyre, a senior ex-consul as the herald would not be inappropriate.[4] Cluvius was a noted orator who did not use his eloquence to prosecute his rivals.[5] Given his family's philhellene tradition, we may guess that he excelled in the display performances of epideictic oratory; such skills would find an ideal outlet in the context of Nero's games.[6]

Appointed by Galba to govern northern Spain (Tarraconensis), he manoeuvred diplomatically in the civil war of 69, transferring his allegiance first to Otho and then to Vitellius. As a man whose expertise was with words, not armies, what else could he do?[7] It evidently did him no harm with Vespasian, the eventual victor, and when peace returned Cluvius Rufus settled down to write history. He was well qualified: consul under Gaius, a conspicuous member of the court of Nero, a prominent, if reluctant, participant in the civil war—and a man who knew what to do with language. For according to Hellenistic theory, historiography was closely related to epideictic oratory, if not actually a subdivision of it.[8]

Our certain knowledge of Cluvius' *Historiae* consists of four fragments and one anecdote. The fragments, numbered as in the new collection of *The Fragments of the Roman Historians*,[9] are as follows:

F1 (Plutarch *Roman Questions* 107, trans. H.J. Rose)

> Why do the Romans call actors *histriones*? Is it for the reason Cluvius Rufus assigns? He declares that in very far-off times, when Gaius Sulpicius and Licinius Stolo were consuls [364 BC], there was a plague in Rome, and the actors died one and all; so at the request of the Romans there came a number of excellent artists from Etruria, of whom the most famous and most successful on the stage was named Ister; wherefore all players were called *histriones* after him.

F2 (Tac. *Ann.* XIII 20.2):

> Pliny and Cluvius report no doubts about the loyalty of the Prefect [Burrus].

F3 (Tac. *Ann.* XIV 2.1–2, trans. A.J. Woodman):

> Cluvius transmits that Agrippina was so carried away by the fervour of retaining her powerfulness that in the middle of the day, at a time when Nero was warm with wine and with banqueting, she quite often offered herself to him in his drunken state, smartly made up and prepared for incest; and that, as those closest to them were already noting their reckless kisses and the blandishments which heralded outrage, Seneca sought from a female some defence against these womanly allurements and sent in the freedwoman Acte, who, tense though she was at the danger to herself and at Nero's infamy alike, was to tell him that their incest had been publicised by his mother's boasting and that the soldiers would not tolerate the command of a perverted *princeps*. [Fabius Rusticus alleged that Nero took the initiative.] But the other authors too have relayed the same as Cluvius.

F4 (Plutarch *Otho* 3.1–2, trans. Bernadotte Perrin):

> The emperor [Otho] did not remember his own private grievances against any man soever, and in his desire to please the multitude did not refuse at first to be hailed in the theatres by the name of Nero, and when statues of Nero were produced in public, he did not prevent it.

Moreover, Cluvius Rufus tells us that 'diplomas', such as couriers are provided with, were sent to Spain, in which the *cognomen* of Nero was added to the name of Otho.

The anecdote is reported by the younger Pliny in a letter about Verginius Rufus, who in 68 had defeated Julius Vindex' insurrection in Gaul:[10]

> Only once in my hearing did he go so far as to make a single reference to what he had done. This was the occasion when Cluvius said, 'You know how a historian must be faithful to facts, Verginius, so, if you find anything in my histories which is not as you would like it, please forgive me.' To this he replied, 'Don't you realise, Cluvius, that I did what I did so that the rest of you should be at liberty to write as you please?'

We do not know on what grounds Cluvius criticised Verginius' action, but the story implies that he was a historian who took his responsibilities seriously.[11]

Even from these few scraps, it is clear that Cluvius used his own experience in his history: presumably Otho's missives to Spain in F4 were addressed to him, and it is reasonable to suppose that he was one of the 'companions' who witnessed Agrippina's behaviour in F3. The item of theatrical history in F1 may come from a digression at the point where Cluvius described the *Neronia,* at which he had been the master of ceremonies. Since Josephus' main source quotes Cluvius as an eye-witness (91f), shows a marked interest in theatrical matters (94f), and takes the same view of Gaius' incest (204) as Cluvius took of Nero's (F3), it is a safe bet that Mommsen was right to identify him as Cluvius himself.

If so, then Cluvius wrote in Latin but included quotations in Greek (92)[12]—a very rare thing in Roman historiography, or indeed in any formal Latin genre, but perhaps not surprising in a writer with Cluvius' family tradition and cultural inclinations.[13]

In 1960, Gavin Townend pointed out that the incidence of Greek quotations in Suetonius' lives of the Caesars is particularly high in the biographies from Gaius to Vitellius; on the basis of Mommsen's identification of Josephus' main source, he inferred that the relevant items in Suetonius all came from Cluvius Rufus.[14] Townend followed up this brilliant insight with a series of close readings of Dio, Tacitus and the scholia to Juvenal which together provide a very substantial—if necessarily hypothetical—addition to the Cluvian corpus.[15] Naturally, not all his suggestions are equally convincing; but his argument deserves serious attention.

If Townend is right, then Cluvius' Caligulan narrative included the wedding banquet of C. Piso and Orestilla, where the emperor took the bride and married her himself (he soon divorced her, but exiled them both when she went back to Piso);[16] it included the scene in the Senate when Gaius, in a set speech, denounced Domitius Afer for some imagined slight, which Afer (himself a master-orator) survived by ostentatiously marvelling at the emperor's oratorical brilliance;[17] it included L. Vitellius' recall from Syria for being too successful, and his escape from a charge of treason by grovelling before Gaius and worshipping him as a god.[18] All three cases exemplify to perfection the analysis of tyranny which Josephus' main source puts in the mouth of Sentius Saturninus (175–81).

Piso, Afer and Sentius, as consuls in the period 39–41,[19] were exact contemporaries of Cluvius Rufus; Vitellius, consul in 34, was a few years older. It is more likely than not that Cluvius witnessed these things himself, and that his history dwelt on the contrasting fortunes of the senators of that generation: Afer, as a prosecutor, and Vitellius, as a courtier, flourished under later emperors,[20] while Piso and Sentius died for opposing Nero.[21] And the aedile whose toga Gaius filled with mud went on to be emperor himself.[22]

Nothing is more conspicuous in Josephus' main source than the contrast between Gaius' autocracy and the liberty of the Republic. Townend's analysis attributes to Cluvius the report of an imperial banquet at which Gaius quoted Homer, 'Nay, let there be one ruler, and one king';[23] and also the description of Helvidius Priscus (who in the Senate in 70 had a generous word for Cluvius Rufus) as both a philhellene and a republican.[24] Moreover, Boudicca's speech on liberty in Dio, also Cluvian according to Townend, has features in common with the speech of Sentius Saturninus in Josephus which suggest the same rhetorical mind at work.[25]

Even the mannerisms of Josephus' main source can be paralleled in Townend's Cluvius-passages. For instance, the unattributed speech in the theatre scene (140) is reminiscent of those in the rhetorical treatment of the second battle of Bedriacum.[26] The mysterious voice at the Senate-house (60f) is heard again at Camulodunum.[27] The imagery of play-acting, twice used of

Julius Lupus (199, 271) and to be expected in so stage-struck a historian as Cluvius Rufus, reappears in the 'farce' (*mimus*) of Nero's arrangement with Otho to share Poppaea Sabina.[28] Finally, we may reasonably detect the same striving for rhetorical *tours de force* in Chaerea's three successive speeches, to Clemens (40–3), to Vinicianus (54–8) and to his colleagues (77–83), as in the three pre-battle speeches of Suetonius Paullinus (one to each of his three legions).[29] Only an expert practitioner could do that without repeating himself.

The evidence is all circumstantial, and so the conclusion can never be final. But I think it is as certain as we could ever expect it to be.

On the basis of his own results, Gavin Townend came to the conclusion that Cluvius Rufus was a 'sensational and polemical writer', 'less scrupulous for sober truth than the elder Pliny'; that 'his work was ... a *chronique scandaleuse,* based mainly on the author's access to court secrets', and that his effect on the historical tradition 'is certainly disproportionate to his good faith as a recorder of historical facts.'[30] Yet the very premise of Townend's analysis was the identification of Cluvius Rufus as the author who quoted Greek—that is, Josephus' main source, an author whose obituary of Gaius (201–11) is conspicuously *un*-sensational, and whom Dieter Timpe, for good reasons, felt able to compare with Tacitus himself.[31] How are we to explain this paradox?

I think Townend's judgement is based on two false assumptions: first, that if a narrative is lurid or scandalous, it is therefore untrue; and second, that only sober annalists deserve to be considered as responsible historians.

It is certainly true that many of Townend's Cluvius items concern adultery in high places, particularly on the part of Gaius' sisters—Livilla with Seneca, Agrippina with Pallas, both of them (and their husbands) with the young Tigellinus.[32] But why should we suppose these reports to be without foundation? That family was not noted for monogamy and self-restraint. Nor is there any reason to doubt the items on Nero—his instructors in vice, his behaviour on the stage, and so on.[33] Cluvius was well placed to know the facts.

Townend's only plausible example of slanderous treatment is the great fire of 64, for which, as he cogently argues, Cluvius held Nero personally responsible.[34] But Townend himself points to the evidence of 'certain ex-consuls' who had caught members of Nero's staff with fire-raising equipment:

it is quite in accordance with Suetonius' common method of indirect
and anonymous reference to his sources that the phrase should conceal
the authority of Cluvius Rufus, a consular of many years' standing, who
was in Rome during that summer.

Cluvius may have been wrong about Nero's responsibility for the fire, but he
evidently had good reasons for his opinion. It was not, as Townend alleges,
merely 'a savage and unfounded libel'.[35]

As for the second fallacy, that is best illustrated by Cicero's letter to L.
Lucceius urging him to write a historical monograph on the years 63–57 BC.[36]
There we have one senior senator writing to another; the subject is very
recent political history, on which Lucceius will bring to bear his personal
experience of the events, and make his own judgement on them (§4). But it
will not be an annalistic history. 'If you give your undivided attention to a
single theme and a single personality, I can envisage even now the greater
scope for rich elaboration' (§2); 'the drama (so to speak) of my experiences
. . . has its various 'acts' and numerous examples of dramatic reversal' (§6).

Lucceius, like Cluvius, was a man of hellenised culture.[37] (All the parallels
Cicero cites in his letter to him are Greek ones.) Roman senator though he
was, it is clear that he would handle his material like an epideictic orator
with his eye on the audience's reaction (§§4–5):

> My experiences will provide you with plenty of variety ... mixed with
> the kind of pleasure which can hold the attention of your readers.
> For nothing is more calculated to entertain a reader than changes of
> circumstance and the vicissitudes of fortune ... The unpredictable
> and fluctuating circumstances surrounding a great figure induce
> admiration, anticipation, delight, misery, hope and fear. And if they
> have a memorable outcome, the reader feels a warm glow of pleasure.

Even an authoritative first-hand witness needs to present his material with
the vividness that will make it come alive for his readers.[38]

That, I think, is what Cluvius did. If Townend's analysis is right, we have
a superb example of his technique in the narrative in Suetonius of Nero's last
hours, clearly drawn from the eye-witness account of one of his attendants.[39]
Equally brilliant is the passage transmitted by Josephus (127–52) of the scene
Cluvius himself witnessed in the theatre in 41. The man who wrote those
things was a literary artist of some stature.

Notes

1 E.g. Cicero *Ad familiares* XIII 56.1; *Inscriptiones Latinae liberae rei publicae* 561; A.J.N. Wilson, *Emigration from Italy in the Republican Age of Rome* (Manchester 1966) 109, 133.

2 Livy XLI 28.5, XLII 9.8; *Inscriptions de Delos* 1679; Dio LII 42.4.

3 See the commentary on Josephus 91; Syme *Tac.* 653–4 on the age for the consulate.

4 Suet. *Nero* 21.1–2, Dio LXIII 14.3.

5 Tac. *Hist.* I 8, IV 43.

6 For *epideixis* as a Greek genre flourishing under Rome (and on prominent display at Greek festival games), see Alex Hardie, *Statius and the Siluae* (Liverpool 1983) ch. 6.

7 Tac. *Hist.* I 8 ('vir facundus et pacis artibus, bellis inexpertus'), I 76, II 65, III 65.

8 Cicero *Orator* 37, 66; Theon, *Rhetores Graeci* II 70.22.ff; A.J. Woodman, *Rhetoric in Classical Historiography* (London 1988) 95–8.

9 Ed. T.J. Cornell (Oxford, forthcoming), at pp. 1039–41. Barbara Levick, whose Introduction (at pp. 549–60) is now the standard work on Cluvius, is doubtful about his identification as J.'s main source (550–1, 554–5).

10 Pliny *Letters* IX 19.5 (trans. Betty Radice), written probably about 107.

11 Cf. Syme *Tac.* 178 on 'judgement and equity'.

12 See also 272, where the word-play depends on the Greek word *acharistia*.

13 For Greco-Roman 'biculturalism', cf. T.P. Wiseman, *Transactions of the American Philological Association* 115 (1985) 187–96, and in *Roman Studies Literary and Historical* (Liverpool 1987) 297–305.

14 G.B. Townend, 'The Sources of the Greek in Suetonius', *Hermes* 88 (1960) 98–120.

15 *Hermes* 89 (1961) 227–48; *Latomus* 20 (1961) 337–41; *Hermes* 92 (1964) 467–81; *American Journal of Philology* 85 (1964) 337–77; *Classical Quarterly* 22 (1972) 376–87.

16 Scholiast to Juvenal 5.109; Townend, *CQ* 1972.378f; cf. Suet. *Cal.* 25.1, Dio LIX 8.7–8.

17 Dio LIX 19.1–6; Townend, *Hermes* 1961.232.

18 Dio LIX 27.2–6; Townend, *Hermes* 1961.230.

19 For Piso, see Edward Champlin, *Museum Helveticum* 46 (1989) 101–24.

20 Tac. *Ann.* IV 52, 66; Suet. *Vitellius* 2.4–3.1.

21 Tac. *Ann.* XV 48–59; *Hist.* IV 7.

22 Dio LIX 12.3 (Vespasian); Townend, *Hermes* 1961.2.34.

23 Suet. *Cal.* 22.1; Townend, *Hermes* 1960.102. (The kings who were present were no doubt Agrippa and Antiochus of Commagene: cf. Dio LIX 24.1.)

24 Schol. on Juvenal 5.34; Townend, *CQ* 1972.378. (Tac. *Hist.* IV 43 for Helvidius' reference.)

25 Dio LXII 3–5 (Townend, *Hermes* 1964.467–9), esp. 3.2, 4.1, 5.1; compare respectively Josephus 173, 180f, 178f.

26 Dio LXV 13.2; Townend, *Hermes* 1964.475–8.

27 Dio LXII 1.2; Townend, *Hermes* 1964.467–9.

28 Suet. *Otho* 3.1–2, Dio LXII 11.2; Townend, *Hermes* 1961.243f.

29 Dio LXII 9–11; Townend, *Hermes* 1964.467–9.

30 Quotations from *Hermes* 1964.470, *Latomus* 1961.338, *AJP* 1964.346, *Hermes* 1961.248 (n. 15 above).

31 Timpe, RG 483–6, 493, 496, 499f.

32 Dio LX 8.5, Schol. on Juvenal 1.109, 1.155, 5.109; Townend, *Hermes* 1961.233, *CQ* 1972.378f.

33 Dio LXII 13.3 (Tigellinus), Tac. *Hist.* I 73 (Calvia Crispinilla), Suet. *Nero* 46.3 (Nero as Oedipus); Townend, *Hermes* 1961. 231, *AJP* 1964.353, *Hermes* 1960.104.

34 Dio LXII 16–17, Suet. *Nero* 38.1; Townend, *Hermes* 1960.111f, cf. 1964.469–71.

35 Townend, *Hermes* 1964.470.

36 Cicero *Ad familiares* V 12; translation and discussion in Woodman, *Rhetoric* (n. 8 above) 70–4.

37 For the family's commercial interests in the Greek East, see J.H. D'Arms, *Commerce and Social Standing in Ancient Rome* (Harvard 1981) 64.

38 On vividness (*enargeia*), see Quintilian VIII 61–81 ('ponere rem ante oculos').

39 Suet. *Nero* 47–9; Townend, *Hermes* 1960.105.

Index of Names